ANCIENT CULTURE AND SOCIETY

THE STOICS

ANCIENT CULTURE AND SOCIETY

General Editor
M. I. FINLEY
*Professor of Ancient History
at the University of Cambridge*

THE STOICS

F. H. SANDBACH

Emeritus Professor of Classics,
University of Cambridge

1975
CHATTO & WINDUS
LONDON

Published by
Chatto & Windus Ltd
40 William IV Street
London WC2N 4DF
*
Clarke, Irwin & Co. Ltd
Toronto

ISBN 0 7011 1735 5 (Hardback)
ISBN 0 7011 1736 2 (Paperback)

Printed in Great Britain by
Cox & Wyman Ltd
London, Fakenham and Reading

CONTENTS

Chronological Table

Since Greek calendars did not coincide with ours some of these dates are slightly uncertain. For example, an event here assigned to 307 may have taken place in the earlier part of 306.

An asterisk distinguishes heads of the Stoic school at Athens.

Leading Stoics	*Important events*
	Death of Aristotle 322
*Zeno of Citium, born *c.* 333 came to Athens 312 died 262	Foundation of Peripatetic School by Theophrastus *c.* 317
Aristo of Chios	Polemo succeeds Xenocrates as head of the Academy 314
Persaeus of Citium at Corinth 243	Epicurus opens school in Athens 307 Arcesilaus head of the (Middle)
*Cleanthes of Assos, died 232	Academy 268 (?) – 241
Sphaerus from the Bosporus at Sparta 235	
*Chrysippus of Soli, born *c.* 280 died *c.* 206	Carneades revives scepticism in the
*Zeno of Tarsus	(New) Academy
*Diogenes of Seleucia (Babylon), died *c.* 152	Carneades and Diogenes on embassy to Rome 155
*Antipater of Tarsus, died *c.* 130	Sack of Corinth by Mummius 146
Apollodorus of Seleucia	Carneades died 129
Archedemus of Tarsus	
Boethus of Sidon	
*Panaetius of Rhodes, born *c.* 185 associated with Scipio and his friends 138(?)–129 died *c.* 110	
Hecato of Rhodes	Antiochus of Ascalon borrows much from Stoicism (Fifth Academy)
*Mnesarchus } Joint heads *Dardanus	Sack of Athens by Sulla 86
Posidonius of Apamea, born *c.* 135, died *c.* 55	Cicero writes on philosophy, mainly in 45 and 44
Seneca the Younger, born AD 1 died AD 65	Augustus, Emperor 23 BC–AD 14
Musonius, banished AD 65 at Rome AD 89	Nero, Emperor AD 54–68 Vespasian, Emperor AD 70–79
Epictetus, opens school at Nicopolis AD 89	
Hierocles	Hadrian, Emperor AD 117–138
Marcus Aurelius, born AD 121 Emperor AD 161–180	

Preface

STOICISM, a philosophical system which originated at the beginning of the third century BC, was an intellectual and social influence of prime importance for five centuries; after that its effects are evident in many Christian writers; and since the Renaissance its teaching has affected both philosophers and thoughtful men in search of a guide to life. In the late nineteenth century the German philosopher Dilthey wrote that it had been 'the strongest and most lasting influence that any philosophic ethic had been able to achieve'.

Not only the ethics of the Stoics but other parts also of their philosophy have been influential, as Dilthey himself did much to show. But it is for ethics that they have been best known and it is about their ethics that we are best informed; accordingly this book emphasises that aspect of their work. To trace their influence in later times is beyond my competence; I have attempted to write about them as they were and to sketch their position in the ancient world.

I have greatly profited from the generous help of several persons, for whose aid I am deeply grateful. My wife and my son made me understand some at least of the needs of readers without a classical background; Professor I. G. Kidd took much trouble over his helpful comments on the section which deals with Posidonius; Mr H. J. Easterling read the whole and offered valuable criticisms and suggestions. Finally Professor Moses Finley's acute and constructive scrutiny of the last draft did much to improve both accuracy and clarity. For faults and errors that remain and for any controversial opinions expressed the responsibility is entirely mine.

F. H. S.

1

Introduction

IN the ancient world of the Greeks and the Romans the words 'philosophy' and 'philosopher' carried different suggestions from those they have today. Literally they mean 'love of wisdom', 'lover of wisdom', and to understand anything at all may be part of wisdom. Therefore the ancient philosopher might venture into fields that are today occupied by specialists, astronomers, meteorologists, literary critics, social scientists and so on. To speak in general terms, they had an insufficient appreciation of the value of experiment and patient observation; a priori reasoning and inference from a few supposed facts were basis enough for explaining the subject in hand. To say this is not to condemn this 'philosophical' activity as useless. Many of its results were mistaken, like most of Aristotle's meteorology, but others were steps in the right direction, like Democritus' atomic theory. Intuitive guesswork has always been one of the methods by which knowledge has advanced. Too often, however, the ancients did not know how to test their guesses, or even that they needed testing.

The modern philosopher agrees with the ancient that ethics belongs to him. But there is a difference. C. D. Broad suggested that a study of ethics would do as little good to a man's conduct as a study of dynamics would to his performance on the golf-links (*Five Types of Ethical Theory* p. 285). Not all philosophers of today would hold such an extreme position, but it is the opposite of that which was all but universal in the ancient world. We study ethics, said Aristotle, not in order to know what goodness is but in order to become good (*Nicomachean Ethics* 1103 b.27). The ancient philosopher, unless he was a sceptic and on principle refused to commit himself, was convinced that ethics had practical consequences; he also held that whatever other subjects he might study, this was the one of first importance. No wisdom could have a higher value than a knowledge of how to live and behave. Some thinkers may have found a more attractive challenge in non-ethical problems, but none could leave ethics aside, the more so because Greek religion, and even more Roman, failed to give adequate guidance. It was largely a matter of ritual, and although not devoid of moral influence, did not offer any coherent set of reasons for the behaviour it encouraged. If any one person can be credited with being the cause of this primacy of ethics, it is Socrates, an Athenian of the later fifth century BC, who exerted a fascination on following generations that is not exhausted even today. He left no writings, but his memory was preserved in the dialogues composed by those who had known him and who made him a character in their works. The figure that appears is of a man who was overwhelmingly interested in discovering the key to right conduct, who by questioning those whom he met forced them to recognise the inadequacy and inconsistency of their thinking on morality, and who hoped to find the answer to his problems by defining the terms of ethical vocabulary, virtue, bravery, justice, and so on. He believed that if one could only know what is good, one could not help but do it; no one was willingly bad, and badness was the result of not knowing what was good. He did not himself claim to have this knowledge; he was only a lover of wisdom (*philosophos*), not a wise man (*sophos*). But he attracted a number of younger men who found intellectual excitement in hearing him discuss, or discussing with him, these problems. Their attachment was increased when in 399 BC he was prosecuted and condemned to death on a charge of 'not recognising the gods recognised by the state, introducing new divinities, and corrupting the young'. The prosecutors no doubt thought that the stability of society was threatened by his influence, which encouraged young men to question traditional assumptions; several of his friends had emphasised the faults of democracy as practised at Athens, and among them the brilliant Critias had in particular excited hatred as leader of the 'Thirty Tyrants', dictators who after Athens' defeat in the Peloponnesian War had with Spartan aid seized power and bloodily maintained it for more than a year.

Socrates' death turned him into a martyr, and far from checking his influence made it grow. Many of his younger friends tried to continue his work and attracted to themselves others who had intellectual interests or a desire to find a rule for life. A large literature came into existence, which represented him as the writers would have had him be. The most important works were the dialogues of Plato, where Socrates is made to carry his spirit of inquiry into subjects, above all psychology and metaphysics, which had never occupied him, and to express views that became more and more positive as time went on. It was probably about 388 that Plato established the body that came to be known as the Academy, because it occupied buildings near the exercise-ground of that name. This was constituted as an association for the worship of the Muses and its members, although no doubt in sympathy with Plato, were independent and sometimes critical of him. Aristotle was among those who worked there; he came as a youth from Macedonia in 367, by no means the only recruit from abroad, and remained until Plato's death twenty years later. He then went to Asia Minor and Macedonia, returning to Athens for the period 335 or 334 to 323 or 322, during which he did some teaching in the Lyceum, another place of exercise.

Meanwhile the Academy flourished under the leadership first of Plato's nephew Speusippus and then of Xenocrates. All the principal figures in it were men of means who could freely devote themselves to philosophical, mathematical, and scientific pursuits, and the young men who came to their lectures or classes were no doubt the sons of well-to-do fathers. Very different was another line of descent from Socrates, who had been a comparatively poor man; his clothes were old and he usually went barefoot. This aspect appealed to Antisthenes, who maintained that wealth and poverty were to be found in the soul not in the purse, and that his own lack of material possessions gave him freedom. He was a copious writer of works, now entirely lost, on a variety of subjects; Aristotle scornfully mentions some of his views on logic. But historically he is important because his writings later stimulated Diogenes, the first of the Cynics, to preach the ascetic manner of life as 'natural' and the way to freedom. Outside Athens Socrates' influence went on in various places, most importantly in Megara, where there was a school of which little is known except that it did important work in logic. Academics, Cynics, and Megarians were all to have their influence on Stoicism.

In the fourth century a young man could choose between two forms of higher education, either rhetoric, that is to say training in the methods of persuasive speech, or philosophy, which was a subject of uncertain scope, depending on the interests of the philosopher to whom he attached himself. But in the Academy it was divided into logic, 'physics' or the study of the physical world, and ethics, which was regarded not as a theoretical subject but one which would have a practical result in right action. The Latin dramatist Terence, translating a play by the Athenian Menander written about the end of the fourth century, makes a father say that 'pretty well all young men have some pursuit: they keep horses or hounds for hunting or go to philosophers ... my son did all these things in a quiet way' (*Andria* 55–7). There was doubtless a large number of men with time on their hands, and many of them will have sampled what philosophers had to offer.

This was the situation when at the end of the fourth century Zeno formed the system of thought that we know as Stoicism. His primary concern was to establish principles to govern conduct; not merely to lay them down, but to show they were right. This involved him and perhaps still more his immediate successors, Cleanthes and Chrysippus, in other subjects which we are inclined to regard as independent and to pursue for their own sakes. The question of right conduct could not be settled without understanding the relation of man to the universe. Seeing him as a single cell, as it were, in a great being with its own life, these Stoics had to attempt to give an account of the processes of that life. Then it was necessary to show that man could have knowledge of the physical world in which he found himself, and how he could correctly develop by reasoning the primary information he obtained. Such questions, in themselves purely intellectual, were embarked on as unavoidable if moral principles were to be securely laid down, but they could in practice be pursued for their own sake.

There is a parallel here with the system of Zeno's slightly older contemporary Epicurus. For him also the centre of philosophy was the question of how one should act. He believed that the only proper object was one's own pleasure, most surely to be attained by a retired and simple life; the greatest obstacles to a pleasant life were anxieties caused by a belief in life after death and that the gods organised or interfered with the running of the world. This led him to give an elaborate account of physical

INTRODUCTION

things, their origin and decay, to argue that all that happens is due to mechanical causes and that death must destroy the soul that gave the body its life. One has the impression that he often took a purely intellectual pleasure in such arguments, and that their ethical bearing was not always prominent in his mind. Similarly with the Stoics, one may suspect that Chrysippus, for example, pursued his investigations into logic because he found them interesting rather than because they were necessary for ethics.

There were men who called themselves Stoics for more than five hundred years. Such a time could not pass without changes. It is unfortunate that the nature of our sources, shortly to be described, does not allow more than a rough account of them.

Of Chrysippus, who worked in the latter half of the third century, it was said that 'if there had been no Chrysippus, there would have been no Stoa'. He seems to have restated, expanded, and to some extent modified the views of Zeno, to have drawn out and accepted even their paradoxical implications, and to have established what can be called an orthodoxy. His successors in the next half-century were mainly concerned to defend this orthodoxy against the attacks of Carneades. The Academy, of which he was head, had already before the time of Chrysippus adopted the sceptical position that nothing could be known, that is known to be certainly true. Carneades was ready to attack any doctrine advanced by other philosophers, but his criticisms fastened particularly on the Stoics. They tried to evade the difficulties by re-phrasing rather than by any real change of meaning. The very fragmentary information that survives about these men suggests that they took a greater practical interest than the more theoretical Chrysippus had done in the kind of problems that arose for decision in real life.

That was certainly true of Panaetius, who was active in the latter part of the second century. What concerned him was not the ideal sage, but the real actual human being in all his variety. He was prepared to re-think and re-fashion his philosophy, taking into account some of the views of Plato and Aristotle, for both of whom he had a high regard. So had his pupil Posidonius, who stands out as a unique figure among the Stoics for the breadth of his studies, which included geography, anthropology, and history, and for his unwavering determination to see knowledge as an integrated whole.

The intellectual energy of Panaetius and Posidonius had no imitators. But in their time and very much through the influence of the former, Stoicism was introduced to the Romans, among whom it was to have its greatest success. At first it had to compete with Epicureanism, and there were intellectuals who were attracted by the suspension of judgment recommended by the Academy. But the Romans tended to be active practical men; many of Cicero's Epicurean contemporaries disregarded their founder's preference for a retired life and his distrust of politics; Cicero himself, professedly an Academic, was deeply affected by Stoicism, being allowed by his sceptical principles to accept views as probable, although they could not be certain. By the end of the first century BC Stoicism was without doubt the predominant philosophy among the Romans, and references to Stoic doctrines, hostile or favourable, are common in Latin literature. There were soon to be Stoic poets, Manilius with his didactic poem on astrology, Persius with his crabbed satires, Lucan with his epic on the civil wars. Although Virgil was an Epicurean as a young man, without Stoicism his *Aeneid* could not have taken the form it has. The Roman lawyers too were powerfully affected, deriving from Stoicism the concept of a law of nature, the product of reason, to agree with which human laws should be adapted.

This influential position was won because Stoicism, while possessing an organised system of thought to support its doctrines, advanced some ideas which met current needs. The belief that the world was entirely ruled by Providence would have an appeal to the ruling class of a ruling people; but it was also a comfort to those for whom things went wrong. To accept misfortune without resentment as something divinely ordered led to ease of mind. Then a man who could rid himself of fear, of cupidity, of anger, as this philosophy commanded, had escaped much cause of unhappiness. It was possible also to derive from it much in the way of practical moral precept. Such aspects seem to have been emphasised at Rome.

In the Greek world of the first two centuries of our era Stoicism clearly remained a lively influence. But this is known more from the controversial writing of opponents like Plutarch,

INTRODUCTION

Galen, and Sextus Empiricus, who undoubtedly have a living tradition in view, than from any information about personalities. Those who are named remain shadowy figures, and there is no evidence that an organised school continued in Athens after the sack of that town by Sulla in 86 BC. But it will hardly be wrong to suppose that alongside a concern for practical morality there persisted an interest in its theoretical justification and in the problems of logic and of the natural world; many of the writings of Chrysippus and his successors of the second century were still available and studied.

But the Stoics of this time whose names are familiar all learned their Stoicism in Rome. Seneca was, however, the only one who wrote in Latin. The oral teaching of Musonius and Epictetus is reported in Greek, and that was certainly the language used by the latter, probably that of the former too. Marcus Aurelius also wrote his *Meditations* in Greek. Greek had for centuries been the language of philosophy, for which Latin was an inferior vehicle, being less flexible and lacking a technical vocabulary. Many educated Romans understood Greek, and so Greek teachers of philosophy had no incentive to master a foreign language.

It is these authors from the Roman world who survive to represent Stoic literature. Although they are one-sided, their personalities come out strongly in their books and secured them many readers until recent times. Very different from one another, they share a common outlook. They have a minimal interest in anything but ethics and see in Stoic philosophy an established system of beliefs that could guide, comfort, and support a man in the difficulties and dangers of life. They are preachers of a religion, not humble inquirers after truth. It was not unusual at Rome for a wealthy family to keep a philosopher, much as great families in England used to keep a chaplain. The philosopher is often called the 'doctor of the soul', and to Seneca he is the 'paedagogus' of the human race, that is the servant who supervised the behaviour of the growing child.

The third century AD brought a sudden decline. The peaceful and prosperous age of the Antonines was succeeded by turmoil, civil war, and a growingly restrictive form of society. New religions, and for the philosophically inclined a revived Platonism, offered the consolations of life after death for the miseries, hard to approve, of this world. But although professed Stoics became few, Stoicism continued to exert its influence. In particular it provided a great deal of material to those members of the Christian church who wished to build up an intellectual structure on their faith. They might absorb it, alter it, or refute it; but in any case they were in part moulded by it.

A difficulty faces anyone who writes about the Stoics: not a single work remains extant that was written by any one of them during the first three hundred years after the foundation of the school. Of Zeno there are two brief quotations which are certainly verbatim and half a dozen more which may be. Of Cleanthes, his successor, there is a little more and more still of Chrysippus, but scraps only, isolated from their contexts. For all three, as for all the Stoics before Panaetius, we depend on information provided by later writers, whether followers or opponents or historians (if they deserve the name) of philosophy. The last were concerned to give in a desiccated form the main outlines of the systems they described, sometimes citing one or more Stoics as authorities for a doctrine, occasionally recording a divergence between their witnesses. Of these writers the most important is Diogenes Laertius, now put in the second century AD. There is part of a rather better work by Arius Didymus, who was a court philosopher to the Emperor Augustus. Aetius' handbook, *Opinions of the Philosophers*, must be used with caution.

The chief of the opponents is Plutarch, who writing before and after the turn of the first century AD provides much information. A confirmed and unsympathetic critic of the Stoics, he was well-informed and did not intend to misrepresent the views he attacked. In the early half of the second century the sceptic Sextus Empiricus made it his practice to expound the doctrines he intended to criticise. Later in the same century the physician Galen, well-read and verbose, found occasion for attacking Chrysippus' psychology at length and supporting that of Posidonius; here and there he provides other pieces of information.

Unique among the non-Stoic authorities is Cicero, who tried to give Greek philosophy a Latin dress to recommend it to Roman readers. Writing very rapidly, not always with full understanding of his models, and using a language which lacked an established philosophical vocabulary, he translated, paraphrased, abbreviated, and expanded Greek authors. Although this led to some distortion, he is indispensable not only because he provides the earliest evidence about the Stoics but also because he writes with verve and feeling, preserving an element lost in cold summaries. His work *On Duties* was based on Panaetius and *On the Nature of the Gods* makes some use of Posidonius, whom he knew personally, but for the most part he seems to be following orthodox sources, as in *On Fate* and the third book of *Goals of Life* (*De Finibus*).

From these varied witnesses one can reconstruct in outline a system which can be called orthodox Stoicism. The main lines were no doubt laid down by Zeno, but Chrysippus filled them out, and some of the details may have been added by later authors. Some points can be recognised over which Chrysippus disagreed with Zeno; they are noticed by our authorities. It is a temptation, but a mistake, for the historian of thought to discover more divergencies; information is too uncertain and inadequate to allow us to find differences that were not noted in antiquity. For the most part Chrysippus was probably expanding and developing rather than altering the doctrines of the founder; his reported saying 'Give me the views and I'll find the arguments' was not a claim to great originality.

The system having been explained, the subsequent chapters of this book consider how later Stoics modified it and selected from it. Many of them are more accessible to us than the earlier thinkers. Their works survive in whole or in part; more is known of their lives and more of the society and circumstances in which they lived. The early Stoics had intended their philosophy to form a guide to life, but the very nature of the evidence makes them appear as theoreticians. Many of the later Stoics were practical men of action and one can see the relevance of their beliefs to their doings. Even those who were primarily teachers were mainly concerned with the practical problems of life which faced them and their pupils.

2

The Founder

AT the north-west corner of the agora, the great central square of Athens, stood the Stoa Poikile or Painted Colonnade, so called from the mural paintings by Polygnotus and other great artists of the fifth century BC that adorned it. Here, in the early part of the third century BC, could often be seen a seated figure talking to a group of listeners; his name was Zeno and his followers, first called Zenonians, were later described as 'men from the Stoa' or 'Stoics'.

Zeno was not an Athenian, but the son of a merchant, Mnaseas, from Citium in Cyprus. Mnaseas, although a good Greek name, was one sometimes adopted by Phoenicians, and Citium, once a Greek colony, was no predominantly Phoenician in language, in institutions, and perhaps in population. Zeno's contemporaries who called him a Phoenician may have been justified in so doing, but he must be imagined as growing up in an environment where Greek was important. His father is said to have brought home from Athens many 'Socratic books', which fired the young man's imagination. Anecdotes of this kind were often invented in antiquity and must always be treated with some reserve, but this one at least has a certain plausibility, and may have been recorded by his pupil Persaeus, with whom he at one time shared a house

It was as a youth of 22 (Persaeus was the authority for this) that Zeno came to Athens in the year 312 or 311 BC. There is an anecdote that he sat down by a bookseller, who was reading aloud from Book II of Xenophon's *Reminiscences of Socrates (Memorabilia)*: he asked where men of that kind were to be found; at that moment Crates the Cynic happened to pass by, and the bookseller replied 'Follow that man'. The story may be merely ben trovato, but there is no doubt that in his early years Zeno did come under Crates' influence, and his first book, the Republic, was said to have been written when he was 'backing up the dog'. 'Cynic' means 'canine', and the first dog had been Diogenes, who was given that nickname because of his shameless behaviour, and who accepted it as being the watch-dog of morality. He was dead before Zeno came to Athens and Crates was the most gifted of his followers. Cynicism was hardly a philosophy; it was more an attitude and a way of life. Diogenes, who had been reduced from affluence to poverty, found a guiding light, as has been said, in the writings of Antisthenes. Right thinking, virtue, and happiness were an indissoluble trio, and material possessions irrelevant. Diogenes tried to show their unimportance by sleeping rough, relying on charity for his food, and having no clothes but a cloak. One of his cries was 'Deface the currency', that is put out of circulation the artificial coinage that passes as valuable:[1] and rules and customs that govern our behaviour in society are nothing but a bondage to be shaken off; we should live as nature commands.

The Cynics had some admirable or at any rate attractive doctrines. To be good is all that matters; to be good brings happiness; to be wise, that is to know how to act, makes one good; one ought to live naturally, and freely. But these are isolated principles rather than a philosophic system; and they assume that anyone can see what constitutes goodness and what a natural life is. 'Virtue', Antisthenes had said, 'is not a thing that needs a lot of talk', and when asked what was the most necessary branch of learning, he had replied 'to unlearn your vices'. Although strongly affected by the Cynic outlook, Zeno could not remain satisfied with it and after a time he became a pupil of Polemo, a man of no great originality, who had succeeded Xenocrates as head of the Academy, the leading philosophical school of the day; here he will have got to know something of Plato's views, as modified, developed, and organised by the master's successors. This is the influence recognised by the scholars of antiquity, and this is the first place to look for the sources of Zeno's thought.

Many modern writers try to find a connexion with Aristotle, but this I believe to be a mistake, due to the tempting supposition that he loomed as large to the generation that succeeded him as he does to us. There is much to suggest that those works

[1]This interpretation is supported by Dio Chrysostom 31.24, Julian *Orations* 7.211c; see also C. T. Seltman, *Proceedings of the Cambridge Philological Society*, cxlii (1929) 7.

of his that are read today, works mostly not prepared for publication, sometimes barely intelligible notes, were for the most part not known until they were edited in the first century BC. There may have been private copies of some made for pupils, but they do not in general seem to have been in the book-trade or to have been part of what philosophers might be expected to read. The only books of his mentioned by early Stoics are two published works, now lost, the *Protrepticus* (*A Call to Philosophy*) and *On Justice*. It is certain that some of his ideas were accepted and used by his pupil Theophrastus, who founded the so-called Peripatetic school shortly before Zeno's arrival in Athens; but although some knowledge of the unpublished Aristotelian doctrine may have thus reached Zeno at second-hand, there is no hint in the ancient sources that the Stoic ever listened to the Peripatetic. The foregoing sentences can give but a partial and inadequate account of the problem, but they must serve to explain why this book leaves Aristotle almost entirely out of account. It is often said that the Stoics 'rejected' this or that characteristically Aristotelian doctrine: it is better to say that they ignored it.

Zeno is reputed to have listened also to Diodorus 'Cronus' and Stilpo, the leaders of the 'Megarian school', who were greatly interested in logical puzzles and the invention of arguments that seemed to lead to paradoxical conclusions. It was, however, probably not this that attracted Zeno, who later found the principal merit of logic in its ability to show the falsity of such constructions, but rather Stilpo's moral teaching, which was not unlike that of the Cynics. He saw the wise man as entirely self-sufficient, needing no friends, quite independent of external possessions: no one could take from him his wisdom, and he was unaffected by the misfortunes that other men would count as evils. It is uncertain when Zeno began to talk in the Stoa or how soon his teaching had taken a form to which the name of Stoicism can properly be given. There was no formal foundation of a school, and the Stoics, unlike the other three groups, Academy, Peripatetics, and Epicureans, had no common property or legal status. One may imagine a gradual process of growth, as Zeno developed his ideas and drew to himself an increasing number of hearers, many from overseas.

THE FOUNDER

The Stoa was a public place where foreigners were as welcome as citizens. But he had Athenians among his audience too. When he died in 262 the assembly passed a resolution to honour him by a tomb and by setting up inscriptions in the exercise grounds of the Academy and the Lyceum, places of education as well as sport. The decree opens with the following words:

> Since Zeno of Citium, son of Mnaseas, has spent many years in the city engaged in philosophy, and in every way has always shown himself a good man, and in particular by exhorting to virtue and good behaviour the young men who came to associate with him has stimulated them to the best of conduct, exhibiting as an example to all his own way of life, which followed what he said in his talk, therefore it has seemed good to the people to praise Zeno of Citium, son of Mnaseas, and to crown him with a golden garland, etc.

This testimonial need not be entirely disbelieved, even although the decree was proposed by one Thraso, the agent at Athens of Antigonus Gonatas, King of Macedon, who was an admirer of Zeno's, had visited him in Athens, and vainly invited him to his court. A few months before Zeno's death Athens had surrendered to Antigonus, starved out by a long siege; and the political independence, for which she had struggled ever since the defeat of Chaeronea (336 BC), had gone, never to be recovered. Stoicism is sometimes represented as a philosophy devised to form a refuge for men disorientated by the collapse of the system of city-states, 'a shelter from the storm'. This is based on a misapprehension. The city-state had never given security, and it remained the standard primary form of social organisation even after military power had passed into the hands of the great monarchies. As a corrective one may quote the words of C. Bradford Welles :

> It is fantasy and perversion to see in Stoicism a new personal doctrine invented to sustain the Greeks in a cityless world of great Empires, for Hellenism was a world of cities, and Hellenistic Greeks were making money, not worrying about their souls. (*Greece and Rome*, 1965, 227.)

At Athens political life continued active and often bloody during almost the whole of Zeno's time. What is true is that during the fifty years following the death of Alexander the Great many Greeks left their own cities hoping, it may be presumed, to find a better life elsewhere. Many went to the new lands of Asia. Men who were looking for a wider cultural life than their own towns could provide would be attracted to Athens. Almost all of Zeno's followers whose origins are known were of this sort; they were people who, like him, had abandoned what rights and duties they may have had in their own cities, preferring the disadvantages of life as aliens, second-class residents, legally, politically, and socially deprived, but enjoying the stimulus of an intellectual ambience.

Some scholars have seen in the real or supposed Semitic origin of several prominent Stoics, in particular of Zeno and Chrysippus, an influence on the development of their thought. It is safer to leave this out of account. Little is known about the intellectual or religious climate in which they grew up, since it cannot have been uniform in all Semitic communities; the Jews and the Carthaginians may have had something in common, but the differences were greater. Nor is it necessary to look for some factor outside Greece : Stoicism can be adequately explained as a natural development of ideas current among the Greeks.

Zeno's first book, now lost like all his other works, was concerned with the structure of society. There has been much dispute about the intention of his Republic, and I give the interpretation that seems to me best to suit the evidence. It laid down how men ought to live together. Only the wise, that is those who think right and therefore act right, do what they ought. Therefore he described a society of the wise, in a sense an ideal society, but not necessarily one that he regarded as impracticable. The proposals were 'relevant to his own place and time' (Philodemus, *Against the Stoics,* xviii). He may have had a young man's optimism about the prospects of reform. Nor need he have supposed that social change must wait until all men were wise: his proposals might be practicable if they were accepted by a large majority in any one place.

To entitle his book *Politeia* (*Republic* or *Political State*) was a paradox, because he swept away everything that the Greeks regarded as characteristic of the *polis* or organised society. There were to be no temples, no law-courts, no 'gymnasia', no money. Wise men are friends, and friends according to the Greek proverb, share their possessions; in a commune of friends there will be no more need for cash-transactions than inside a family. Gymnasia, not only exercise-places, but also the scene of 'higher education', were an aid to political life, which was also prosecuted in the courts of law; political struggles and legal framework have no value for men who know how to live together. Temples and statues of gods were the visible symbols of national unity; but the wise man will set no store by them, having a lofty contempt for the products of the manual workers' hands. Plutarch wrote (*Moralia* 329 A) that Zeno's *Politeia* can be summarised as saying that 'we should not live organised in cities or in demes,[1] each group distinguished by its own views of right, but should think all men our fellow-demesmen and fellow citizens, and that there should be one way of life and one order, like that of a flock grazing together on a common pasture' (or 'under a common law'). The word *nomos* used in the Greek can mean either 'pasture' or 'law', but even if the latter interpretation is correct, the intention was not that there should be any organised world state, but that wherever men came together they should be governed by the rule of reason, which would be the same the world over. Other reports represent Zeno as speaking of what should be done in cities; he must have meant thereby not 'political' cities, but 'physical' cities, groups of men living in the same place.

Opponents of Stoicism were to make play with Zeno's proposals in this book with regard to sex. He is said to have favoured 'community of wives' or that 'any man should lie with any woman'. This was later accepted and defended by Chrysippus, the third head of the school, who explained that the children would be cared for by their elders in general and that incest was not unnatural, being common among animals. It is likely enough that Zeno had advanced the same considerations. But his reasons for advocating this sexual permissiveness, which extended to homosexual acts, are less certain. Chrysippus was

[1] A deme was a subdivision of a city, with many important functions in society.

to say that community of wives would avert the jealousy caused by adultery; but a society of wise men would be in no danger of feeling jealousy. More probably Zeno took over the attitude of the Cynic Diogenes, who had in his *Republic* gone even further, approving all forms of coition. This had been part of his campaign to return to nature and cast off the conventions with which man had impeded himself. But to Zeno it may have seemed that in a society of wise men and wise women monogamy would serve no purpose. In actual societies marriage usually provided a home where children could be brought up, while husband and wife were a mutually supporting pair. Among the wise, however, charity would not begin at home: there benevolence would extend equally to all the human race; there would therefore be no need for the particular protection afforded by the household. In the real world in which the Stoics lived the situation was different, and marriage and the rearing of children came to be approved. Even a wise man, if there were one, some were to say, would see it as right to marry.

Of Zeno's later works little is known but the titles. These include *On the Universe, On Substance, On Vision,* but predominantly they suggest a concern with human behaviour, e.g. *On Life that accords with Nature, On Impulse, On Human Nature, On Passions, On Appropriate Action, On Law, On Greek Education.* He also wrote five books of *Homeric Problems* as well as about Hesiod's *Theogony,* no doubt accepting the popular view that the poets were teachers whose views were to be discovered by interpretation. At times he would rewrite verses if he disapproved their sentiment; for example he amended Sophocles' lines

> 'Who traffics with a tyrant is his slave,
> Although he comes as free'

by writing '——is no slave, Given he comes as free'. He is also the central figure of many anecdotes, which testify to his being a man who caught people's attention. Several show him as putting down presumptuous young men. To a talkative youth he said, 'We have one tongue and two ears to listen twice as much as we speak'. Such reproof and even more biting ones earned him a reputation for harsh severity alongside the respect that was paid to his self-control and simple manner of life.

By his oral teaching and in his written works Zeno must have laid down the outlines of the system we call Stoicism. But it is impossible to draw a firm line between his contribution and those of his successors. All that can be done in a book of this size, at least, is to give an account of orthodox Stoicism, with some reference, where the sources allow, to the founder or to other individual members of the school.

3

The System: Ethics

Central to the Stoic system of ethics was the view that what was morally perfect, virtue (*aretê* in the narrow sense of the word[1]) and acts and persons that were virtuous, belonged to a class of its own, incomparable with anything else; that to be virtuous was the same as to be happy; that 'good' (*agathon*) was an absolute term applicable only to moral perfection. This alone always had effects of which a wise man would approve: everything else which ordinary speech called good, e.g. wealth, health, intelligence, might be used for bad purposes, to commit wicked acts. Virtue, too, was an absolute term: it was a state such that its possessor would always do what was right,[2] and this was possible only if he always knew what was right: hence the virtuous man must be a wise man, and virtuous because he was wise. By a symmetrical process of reasoning the word 'bad' (*kakon*) must be restricted to what was morally imperfect, and most of the things that were in ordinary speech called 'bad', e.g. death, ill-repute, and ugliness, should not be given that name, since they did not necessarily lead to wickedness, but might be the material for virtuous action. All such things like those that were popularly called 'good' were *per se* morally indifferent (*adiaphora*).

[1] *Aretê*, conventionally translated 'virtue,' had a wider sense, more like 'excellence'. But, as used by the Stoics and often by philosophers contemporary with them, it denoted what we may call moral excellence, with the proviso that it included an intellectual element of understanding or knowledge. Hence the possessor of virtue, the good man, is also a 'wise man'. It was then assumed that other forms of excellence need not be taken into account: this moral excellence and human excellence were treated as identical.

[2] There was a dispute whether virtue, once acquired, could be lost again. Cleanthes said no, Chrysippus more cautiously said that intoxication or madness might cause its loss. The question is not worth recording except as an example of the unprofitable speculation into which philosophers could be led.

Goodness, however, and knowledge, although they had value of a unique kind, could not be the only things to have value. Right action was a matter of choice concerned with morally indifferent things—will you look for wealth or accept poverty, marry or remain a bachelor, live or die?—and choice between absolutely indifferent alternatives would not involve knowledge or reason. A man who says that goodness is knowledge may be asked: knowledge of what? If he answers that it is knowledge of goodness, the reply is unilluminating and involves an eternal regress. Zeno escaped from this by recognising that things morally indifferent were yet not without degrees of value or its opposite. He said that just as at a court the king was in a class of his own, *sui generis,* but the courtiers had their ranks of precedence, so the good was unique, but among things morally indifferent some were preferred to others. In general health, wealth, and beauty, would be preferred by a sensible man, if he had the choice, rather than sickness, poverty, or ugliness. Virtue can then consist in the effort to obtain these things that have value and to avoid their contraries, and knowledge can be knowledge of what is to be preferred. But since things of this sort are not good or bad, it is of no importance whether one has them or does not have them, so far as goodness is concerned. The good intention is enough; achievement may be impeded by forces outside a man's control.

Zeno held moreover that virtue or goodness was the sole cause of *eudaimonia* or happiness: the reasons for this opinion will be discussed later; but if it is accepted, there is a striking result: happiness is not in any way forwarded by possession of things that, although preferable, are morally indifferent. Nor is it in any way spoiled if one is saddled with their opposites, for they do not prevent one from being morally good, and that is the only way to be happy. Throughout the history of Stoicism this is a key-point and one perhaps of increasing importance. A man's excellence or virtue—the Greek word *aretê* covers both—does not depend on his success in obtaining anything in the external world, it depends entirely on his having the right mental attitude towards those things. The external world should not be a matter of indifference to him, and he is bound to recognise differences of value in it, but they are not values that contribute to his excellence and his happiness, of which he is the sole arbiter. The self-confidence and self-reliance which this belief gave to the Stoic were of immense help to many men in facing the dangers and misfortunes of life. Whether the belief is justifiable, is another question. And even for the Stoics there were difficulties in associating it with other beliefs that they held. This will appear later, on further inspection of the ideas involved.

For the moment it is enough to see how they insisted upon the cleft between the morally good and the morally indifferent, and between the values that attached to the two classes. The contrast was marked by a vocabulary which was carefully maintained. The morally good was 'to be won' (*haireton*), the morally bad 'to be fled from' (*pheukton*), the indifferent was either 'to be taken' (*lêpton*) or 'picked' (*eklekteon*) or 'not to be taken' (*alêpton*). It is imposible to find a set of English adjectives that will correctly represent the Greek words. I shall use 'acceptable' and 'chosen' of the indifferent things that have value; but it must be remembered that choice does not imply that one is committed to getting what is chosen. One should mind only about what is good, i.e. morally good. The foregoing words signify the correct attitude towards the two classes; another set represents their effects. The morally good is 'beneficial' (*ôphelimon*) or 'useful' (*chrêsimon*), the bad 'harmful' (*blaberon*), indifferent things are either 'serviceable' (*euchrêsta*) or 'unserviceable' (*dyschrêsta*). The two kinds of value, that of the morally good and that of the indifferent, are incomparable. One might find a parallel in the difference between counters, which have a value for a game, and money, which has a value for buying groceries. Indifferent things have a value for a natural life, good things value for a moral life.

It was justifiable to argue that of all the things which the ordinary man calls good, those that are morally good stand in a class of their own and should therefore have their own name. The Stoic was then at liberty to say that he would call them good, confining that word to this use, and employ bad only of moral evil. But he was not entitled to say, as he did, that because a thing was not good or bad (in his sense of the words), it had not the qualities normally indicated by those words. By a bad thing men mean something that is to be feared, regretted, or resented. The Stoic argued as follows: 'what you call a bad thing is often not bad (in my sense of the word); for example poverty, illness, the loss of loved ones are not bad; therefore they are not to be feared or resented'. But this is a *non-sequitur*, for it has not been proved that nothing except what is morally bad should arouse these emotions. The assumption that this is true depends upon a confusion. Everyone would accept the statement 'only what is bad is to be feared or resented', if bad is used in its normal manner; the Stoics unjustifiably took it for granted that 'nothing that is not morally bad is to be feared and resented'.

WHAT IS A NATURAL LIFE?

Among the things that were morally indifferent those that had considerable worth were said to 'have precedence' (*proêgmena*), those with considerable 'unworth' were 'relegated' (*apoproêgmena*). Nothing is heard of those with slight worth or unworth; presumably men have more important things to occupy themselves with. This worth or value was relative to the leading of a 'natural' life or as the Stoics put it, a life 'in accord with nature'; for this can be promoted by everything which our sources represent as having precedence: life as opposed to death, health, beauty, strength, wealth, good reputation, good birth, natural ability, technical skill, moral progress, soundness of limb and of the senses, absence of pain, good memory, an acute mind, parents, and children. But this is not value for a moral life; a man is not made good by the possession of any of these things; even the progress of one who is making headway towards being good does not make him good.

The ambiguity of the Greek word *physis*, translated 'nature', caused much difficulty to ancient thinkers, and it has created trouble for critics and historians of Stoicism. Literally the word means 'growth', then 'the way a thing grows', and by extension 'the way a thing acts and behaves'. By a further extension it came to mean 'the force that causes a thing to act and behave as it does'. For the Stoics this force was something material, a constituent of the body it controls; it was found both in plants and in animals. Each individual animal has its own *physis* or way of growing and behaving, and by this is to be understood the way normal for members of its species. Thus it is part of the *physis* of a man to be able to see and hear. If he is blind

31

or deaf, that is contrary to his *physis*, against his nature. But *physis* also governs the whole world, since that too was believed to be a living being. The *physis* of the world is identical with God, the immanent controlling force, and itself material; it is a 'fire that is an artificer, proceeding methodically to bring thing into being'. (See below pp. 73, 79.) The blindness or deafness of the man is then part of the behaviour of that great animal the world, in which he is, in modern language, a single cell: it is therefore, in accord with the world's nature.

Now although the Stoics drew a clear distinction between a natural and a moral life, they would have hotly denied that a moral life was unnatural. For although human nature in a narrow sense means that a man has certain physical abilities, that he can procreate children, associate with friends, and so on, and a natural life is one in which he has and uses these capacities, yet his nature has also endowed him with reason, and it is on reason that a moral life is founded. This is therefore in its own way also a natural life. Moreover it would be wrong to see in it a life opposed to what was first called a natural life; rather it was regarded as a development, as appears from the account which was given of the growth of a man's consciousness of himself.

This account, probably orthodox doctrine and probably propagated by Chrysippus, starts from the concept of *oikeiôsis*, a word for which there is no adequate English translation. *Oikeion* is the opposite of *allotrion*, what is alien; it is therefore that which 'belongs to you', so that you and it go together. *Oikeiôsis* is then the process of making a thing belong, and this is achieved by the recognition that the thing is *oikeion*, that it does belong to you, that it is yours. Sometimes translators use the words 'dear' and 'endearment', but although this idea is present, those of 'belonging' and 'affinity' are stronger, and these latter terms will be employed in this book.[1]

Diogenes Laertius (7. 85) records the Stoic doctrine as follows:

They say that an animal's first impulse is to self-preservation, since Nature from the very first gives it a feeling of affi-

---

[1] S. G. Pembroke in *Problems in Stoicism* ed. A. A. Long p. 116 uses 'concern' and 'make well-disposed'.

nity (*oikeiousês*) to itself, as Chrysippus says in Book I of his *Goals of Life*, where he declares that the first thing that belongs to any animal is its own constitution and consciousness thereof.[1] It is not likely that she would alienate the animal from itself, nor that she would make it and then neither alienate it nor give it a feeling of affinity. One must therefore assert the remaining possibility, namely that having constituted it she gives it this feeling towards itself. That is why it pushes away what is harmful and welcomes what belongs to it.

They show the falsity of the claim made by some people, that the first impulse of animals is towards pleasure: they say that pleasure, if it occurs, is an aftermath, when nature has of her own accord looked for what is fitted to the animal's constitution and obtained it; it is like the sleekness of animals or the thriving of plants.

Nature makes no distinction between plants and animals at the times when she manages the latter as she does the former without employing impulse and sensation, and even in man there are some functions of a vegetable kind. But animals have impulse over and above their vegetable functions, and making use of it they move to obtain that which is properly theirs; and so for them what is natural is to act according to their impulse. But since rational beings have been given reason, to live correctly according to reason becomes natural for them. For it supervenes as a craftsman to control impulse.

It appears then that man's nature from his birth directs him towards the acquisition of certain things that promote his survival and proper constitution. When he acquires reason, which happens spontaneously by the age of fourteen, he begins to modify these primitive impulses; since reason is a gift of nature, this modification is also natural. But he is also

[1]The Greek is uncertain and unsatisfactory. Although the animal may be conscious of its own constitution and feel that consciousness to be something that 'belongs to it', it is not made plain what conclusion follows from that feeling. In a somewhat similar passage of Cicero the child is said to be conscious of itself and therefore fond of itself (*De Finibus* 3.16).

conscious of his rationality; his constitution is no longer the same as it was when he was an infant; it is this new rational constitution and all that goes with it that he now feels to belong to him. He now knows his affinity to morality and to wisdom.

There is another way in which the promptings of nature are extended as a man becomes adult. He is concerned not only with his own survival, but also with that of his race; he has a love of his offspring and an instinct to care for them that can be seen in other animals also. But nature also gives him a desire to live with and help other men; simple forms of this desire for association can be seen in some animals. These feelings and instincts presuppose a recognition that these other people 'belong to us', are ours. Hierocles, an orthodox Stoic of the second century AD (see also p. 170), drew a picture of a man at the centre of a number of concentric circles. In the innermost he stands himself, with his body, and the satisfaction of his physical needs, in the next are his parents, brothers, wife and children, then more distant relations, then members of his deme (ward or village), of his city, of neighbouring cities, of his country, of the human race. Hierocles suggests that we should try to contract the circles, treating e.g. uncles like parents: the ultimate aim would be to treat all men as our brothers.[1] This has been interpreted as a process of coming to feel that the members of each circle in turn belong to us. Elsewhere certainly he speaks of *oikeiôsis* to one's relatives and Cicero makes his champion of Stoicism recognise a natural *oikeiôsis* to all mankind (*De Finibus* 3.63). But it has been objected that it is superfluous to suppose a progress through these circles to a final recognition of affinity with all men, since there are many passages which indicate a belief that man has a natural tendency to love and assist his fellows, from which his *oikeiôsis* to them can be immediately derived. There is no difficulty in this, if there can be degrees of *oikeiôsis*, if it can be felt that where A and B both belong to us, A belongs more than B does. Then recognition of some sort of affinity to any human being may arise without passing through the intermediate stages between him and one's family, but to pass through them

[1]Stobaeus 4 pp. 671–3 Hense.

may be a way to feeling him to belong to one as much as does one's brother.[1]

Here is one way in which the original self-regarding impulses can be modified, as the self is seen to be a part of larger families of men. But there is another way in which man's reason must shape his impulses. The Stoic knows that the world is ordered throughout by the will of God, and that all that happens is part of a single plan. He knows this by faith rather than by argument, although the account which he gives of the physical constitution of things necessitates it. That will be explained later (pp. 72f.) and the difficulties to which this belief gives rise will be examined. But for the moment it is enough to say that an omnipotent and provident deity controls all events. Now it is clear that whereas men aim at what is 'natural' for them, for example to be healthy and to stay alive, sometimes they fall sick and finally all men die. Their illnesses and their death, although apparently contrary to their own individual nature, must nevertheless be part of the whole scheme of things, that is must be in accord with the nature of the world as a whole. Man's reason enables him to recognise that there is this supreme plan, and he can willingly submit himself to it. He will prefer to be healthy and he will act to secure health, because that is the way he is made. But if he falls ill, he knows that this is 'natural' in the wider sense, to be accepted and even welcomed. His

[1]Some scholars have maintained that the doctrine of *oikeiôsis* originated with Theophrastus. Certainly the word occurs once in a fragment (190 Wimmer; not a verbatim quotation), which says that the bee has an *oikeiôsis* to the oak-tree. But this does not imply any general principle, or that man recognised first himself, then external things and persons as 'belonging to him'. The process of growing self-awareness and extending recognition of one's relation to others seems to be a purely Stoic development. Theophrastus claimed that men were akin to one another and also to animals (Porphyry, *On Abstinence* 3.25), but this *oikeiotês* (his word) is no more than an objective physiological and psychological fact, not a feeling of relationship. Arius Didymus ascribes *oikeiôsis* in the Stoic sense to 'Aristotle and the Peripatetics', but in a passage full of Stoic terms and concepts: this came to him from Antiochus, who held that in the main Peripatetics and Stoics had the same views, both derived from Plato. I have no doubt that recent writers are correct in holding that *oikeiôsis* first became important in the Stoa.

reason enables him to transcend his own personal interest and see his own suffering as serving a wider purpose. Chrysippus said:

> So long as the coming sequence of events is not clear to me I always cling to those things that are better adapted for getting what is natural (i.e. natural for me as an individual), since God himself has made me a creature that picks such things. But if I knew that it was fated for me to fall ill now, I should be bent on that. If the foot had brains, it would be bent on getting muddy (quoted by Epictetus, *Discourses* II.6.9).

The sense of the last sentence is that the foot is part of a man, who wishes for his own good reasons to pass through some mud: a rational foot would co-operate, although it would not be to its own advantage to get muddy. Similarly man is part of the world and should co-operate to serve the world's purposes against his own advantage. But this is not against his own good. His good is achieved by rational decision, and reason demands that he should co-operate. Illness is not to his advantage, but he cannot be good unless he accepts his illness. (This does not imply that he should make no attempt to recover; a fated illness is not necessarily a fatal one.)

Illness is usually unexpected, but death can often be foreseen. It was therefore consonant with the Stoic position if both Zeno and his successor Cleanthes, as is reported, and later Antipater hastened their own deaths: they saw that their time had come, and therefore did not fight for life.

The Stoic view may be briefly summed up as follows. Virtue consists in the right approach to things and actions that are in themselves morally indifferent. Some of these have a value, which must however not be exaggerated, others the opposite, an 'unworth', which must equally not be exaggerated: such things are not good or bad. The right approach to what has value will be a positive one, namely to accept it and to act so as to get it; the reaction to what has unworth will be correspondingly negative. But this is not an absolute rule. What may be called the primary interests of the individual sometimes conflict with those of the larger community constituted by the whole world: then he ought to disregard usual values and gladly accept what has 'unworth' for him. Yet this unworth is unimportant, for it attaches to what is contrary only to the lower aspect of his nature; his higher, fully-developed nature is marked by possession of reason, which must, if perfect, coincide with the reason that rules the world, and sometimes allots to him experiences unwelcome in themselves, but acceptable as part of the universal plan.

Cleanthes wrote some verses that well express one element of the attraction that could be exerted by his faith:

> Lead me, O Zeus, and lead me thou, O Fate,
> Unto that place where you have stationed me:
> I shall not flinch, but follow: and if become
> Wicked I should refuse, I still must follow.

Seneca turned these four lines into five of more vigorous and epigrammatic Latin, beginning

> Lead me, father, ruler of high heaven,
> Where you have wished: obedience knows no stay,

and ending

> Fate leads the willing, drags the recusant.

The whole world is ruled by God and nothing in it happens without its being his will. So the good man will accept everything, knowing that it is not only unalterable, since Fate determines all, but also the work of God, the perfect being. Seneca makes him our father, which suggests that he is benevolent. To repine or resist is then folly, for nothing will prevent his will's being done. One may go along with it in willing contentment, or be carried kicking and groaning, in wickedness and misery. This acceptance of all that happens will bring man peace of mind and protection against whatever he may suffer.

Cleanthes' lines say nothing of the other comfort that is offered to the Stoic, namely that his happiness depends entirely upon himself, and is not at the mercy of other persons or the play of outside forces. What brings happiness is to have the right attitude, to choose the right actions, to aim correctly at the mark. This is in the man's own power: success, in the popular meaning of the word, is not. Unforeseen and incalculable causes may prevent his hitting the target, his actions may be obstructed, his attitude disregarded; but so long as he does all he can and has nothing with which to reproach himself, all is well with him. Whether this is reconcilable with absolute determinism is a difficult question; but for a strong character it is a welcome challenge to be told that he must rely upon himself and that self-reliance is the road to happiness.

Two objections

Here it will be convenient to consider two objections that were raised in antiquity. A pupil of Zeno's, Aristo from Chios, argued that among morally indifferent things there are none that always have precedence. For example, whereas health often has precedence over sickness, a wise man would prefer sickness if its result would be to avoid service under a tyrant and consequent death. He went on to allege that things are given precedence simply in accordance with circumstances, and that none are in themselves such that they have a natural advantage; they are like the letters of the alphabet, of which none is superior to any other, but which are chosen in accord with the word we wish to spell. Now, whereas it may be true that none of the things with precedence is always to be taken and accepted, it does not follow that none has any value in itself: it may occur that something which has precedence and value cannot be taken simultaneously with another thing of even greater value; health and life are both things with precedence, but in the situation imagined by Aristo they are alternatives. His mistake stems from supposing that a thing that has value must always be accepted, whereas the world is not so constituted that we can always take at once everything valuable that is open to us.

Ancient critics attacked Aristo in a different way, saying that his position robbed virtue of content; Cicero, probably following Antiochus (p. 120), repeatedly claims that virtue is abolished and that man has no way of ordering his life, unless value attaches to things that are in themselves morally indifferent. There is some exaggeration in this, since Aristo, like any Stoic, believed that it was virtuous not to yearn after or to fear things which were morally indifferent or to feel pain or joy at their presence. But the absence of these faulty emotions is merely negative: there are many occasions when a man must choose between positive courses of action; what can guide him to take one or the other, if their results have no value *per se*? 'You will live magnificently', Cicero reports Aristo as saying, 'you will do whatever seems good to you, without pain, desire, or fear'. Elsewhere he explains this to mean that the wise man will do whatever comes into his head (*De Finibus* 4.69, 4.43). It has been maintained that this is a misinterpretation: in reality the wise man will make his choice after considering all the circumstances in the light of correct reason. Perhaps that was Aristo's view, but if it was, it was impracticable. For one thing, life is too short; for another, if nothing but virtue has value *per se*, the temporary value of other things must be due to their promoting virtue and negative value to their encouraging vice. But usually they will be quite irrelevant in these regards. No one avoids the mutilation of his fingers because a damaged hand will make him morally worse.

Aristo, who had a picturesque style, won a circle of supporters. He greatly simplified Stoicism, so that it was hardly distinguishable from the attitude of the Cynics. He rejected the study of logic as useless, that of physics as beyond human capacity. Like the Cynics he must have thought that virtue and vice were easily recognisable, right and wrong obvious. But unlike Crates he did not think it the philosopher's business to give detailed advice; if a man knew that virtue was the only thing for which he should care, he needed no one to tell him how to behave towards his wife or his father. His 'school' did not survive long, its doctrinal weakness being too evident; yet some of his books were still read four centuries later by the young Marcus Aurelius (*Letters of Fronto* 4.13).

The other objection had longer currency, and is still made. If it is good to live 'in agreement with nature', why is the attainment of so many 'natural' things quite immaterial to a good life and to happiness? They include all the 'primary natural things', to use a phrase that Zeno adopted from his Platonist teacher Polemo. What exactly this covered may never have been defined, but the term included health, strength, powers of sensation, perhaps beauty and physical comfort. Aristotle had been unable to accept the complete irrelevance of the possession of such things; he felt it to be a paradox if a man whose circumstances were extremely disadvantageous could be called happy. Later Antiochus was to maintain that whereas virtue was adequate to make a man happy, his happiness would be increased by the possession of these primary natural things, and something similar seems to have been the position of Polemo. These views are those of common sense.

In defence of the Stoics it may be said that the man who 'lives in accord with nature', that is with the plan of the universe, does not do violence to his own nature. For that nature is rational and directs him sometimes to accept what is contrary to his primary, that is undisciplined, natural impulses. It is clear that it may not be possible to pursue all the instigations of nature simultaneously: one might, for example be able either to protect one's children or to preserve one's health but not both. Similarly, on occasion to follow the purposes of universal nature, with which man's developed nature is in accord, may exclude the simultaneous following of other aspects of his nature. Nor are these other aspects to be seen as opposed to universal nature. Man's nature is part of universal nature and he has been provided with tendencies towards what is normally suitable for him to have. There is no reason why life according to nature should not for the most part mean a life that brings what is 'primarily natural'. But since these tendencies are, as it were, generalised and therefore not always adapted to particular circumstances, man should employ his reason to bring them under control, and to shape them so that his life is in harmony with nature as a whole.

But when this has been said, it remains true that it is strange if the possession of primary natural things is irrelevant to happiness. If they have value *per se*, that ought to affect a man's well-being. Is not X, who is virtuous, healthy, and blessed with admirable children, in some way better off than Y, who is virtuous, sick, and childless? Should we not be right to call him happier? Perhaps we should, but unfortunately the question at issue between the Stoics and their critics was not that, but whether he was more *eudaimon;* and 'happiness', conventionally used as a translation of *eudaimonia*, is (like *eudaimonia* itself) an ambiguous word and none of its meanings a true rendering. Some philosophers make it mean 'balance of pleasure over pain'; the ordinary man may use it of a feeling of satisfaction that can be transient. But *eudaimonia,* although something experienced by the man who is *eudaimon*, is (perhaps primarily) something objective, that others can recognise—having a good lot in life. 'Call no man happy till he die', because one who is apparently enjoying a good lot may be doing so only temporarily: things may yet go wrong. Thus the Stoics did not attempt to describe *eudaimonia* as a subjective feeling, but identified it with such things as 'living a good life', 'being virtuous', or 'good calculation in the choice of things that possess value'. Similarly in the *Book of Definitions* which originated in the Academy *eudaimonia* is not only 'a good compounded of all goods', but also 'a self-sufficient capacity for living well', or 'perfection in virtue'. For the Stoic, who confines the word 'good' to the morally good, it is consistent that a good life is a morally good life and the well-being indicated by *eudaimonia* is unaffected by what is morally indifferent, however acceptable.

To the other philosophers, who do not so restrict the word 'good', *eudaimonia* must be so affected. The basic matter in dispute is whether there is some category that includes not only virtue but also health, wealth and so on. Popular speech, calling all these things 'good', places them in a single category; they can be added like pence and pounds. To the Stoic they are diverse and can no more be added together than inches and pounds be. Health and virtue both have value, but their values cannot be summed, just as both inches and pounds are measures, but a measure of length cannot be summed with a measure of wealth.

VIRTUE

Virtue could be described in many ways, for example as 'an even tenor of life that is always consistent', but it was essentially for the Stoics, as it had been for Socrates, a matter of knowledge or wisdom. In this intellectualist approach they followed not only the Cynics, but also the tradition of the Academy, which held that a man who fully knows what is right must also do it. The Cynics had insisted that knowledge could not be a firm possession without strength of mind, and that strength of mind was to be secured by practice and training: by holding to the truth under temptation a man made himself more capable of holding to it again. The Stoics did not adopt the practices of self-mortification to which this had led Diogenes, but they recognised that habituation was necessary if virtue was to be acquired. Plato had believed that there were irrational forces in men which they must control before they could reach that sort of knowledge which would guarantee virtuous action. This the Stoics did not accept, holding that the road to virtue was that of training the reason to think correctly. When Zeno therefore wished to define the four cardinal virtues, established by the Platonic tradition, he expressed three of them in terms of the fourth, wisdom: justice was wisdom concerned with assignment (or distribution), sophrosyne (self-control, temperance) was wisdom concerned with acquisition, bravery wisdom concerned with endurance. How he defined wisdom itself is not recorded, but later it was called 'knowledge of what should and should not be done' or 'knowledge of what is good or bad or neither'.[1]

Zeno's pupil Aristo argued, with some plausibility, that it would be logical to believe in a single virtue, knowledge of good and evil, given different names according to the field in which it operated. It was as if we called sight 'albivision' when directed towards white objects, 'nigrivision' when directed towards black; we do in fact call the same coin by different names, a 'fare' or a 'fee' or a 'deposit', according to the purpose for which it is used. Cleanthes said that if a *psychê*, that is to say the 'spirit', conceived as a physical 'breath', which gives a man life and reason, was taut enough (see p. 76), it had a strength which was self-mastery when steadfastness was concerned, bravery when endurance, justice when deserts, temperance when acquisition and avoidance. By removing wisdom from the list of cardinal virtues he seems to have wished to avoid the awkwardness of Zeno's scheme, which is most naturally interpreted in Aristo's manner. In this revised scheme each virtue could be different by a modification in the tension of the *psyche*: but that is no more than a guess at his meaning.

Chrysippus attacked Aristo's position at length, preserving

[1]These alternatives illustrate the fact that the word *phronêsis*, translated 'wisdom', covered both theoretical and practical wisdom, both knowledge of what is or exists and of what ought to be done. Its limitation to practical wisdom was an Aristotelian move, and even he recognised that practical wisdom was not independent of theoretical, which he called *sophia*.

the traditional cardinal virtues and maintaining that they could be distinguished by their own characteristics and not merely by the fields in which they operated. Galen devoted many pages to denouncing his arguments as bad ones, without revealing what they were. But he is known to have asserted that each virtue was a different state of the 'breath' which constituted the *psyche*. Nor was he content to distinguish four virtues: there were minor virtues within each of the cardinal virtues, a whole swarm of them, as Plutarch complained.

Yet, although the virtues were different, they implied one another, and could not exist separately. All depended on the knowledge of what was good and bad, and a man who had that knowledge must possess all the virtues. Chrysippus even said that every virtuous action involved every virtue, an opinion that it would be hard to maintain: perhaps it is to be seen as a paradoxical sharpening of the truth that some virtuous actions involve all four cardinal virtues.

Chrysippus enjoyed paradox. Sometimes it was a question of pushing principles to what seemed a logical extreme. Thus he probably said that if any wise man anywhere stretched out his finger wisely, the action was useful to all wise men everywhere. This depends on three principles: all wise men are friends to one another; friends have all things in common, what belongs to one belongs to all; any wise action is useful to the man who performs it. But many of the paradoxes about the wise, for which the Stoics became notorious, were dependent on the use of a word in an unusual sense. They made statements startlingly false, if taken to be in ordinary language, but which could be true with another interpretation. Thus the wise man is a rich man, not in money but in what is truly valuable, the virtues; he is beautiful, not with physical beauty but with that of the intellect; he is a free man, even if a slave, because he is master of his own thoughts. He alone is a king: for by 'king' is meant an ideal ruler, who must know what is good and evil. He alone is a prophet, a poet, an orator, a general, for he alone knows how to follow these professions as they should be followed to achieve acceptable results. The other side of the medal is that every man who is not wise is a slave, to his fears and cupidities; a madman, for his beliefs are hallucinations; a wretched man, for he has no true cause for joy. Nothing is useful for him, nothing belongs to him, nothing suits him; for nothing is useful but virtue, which he lacks, nothing belongs unless it cannot be taken away, nothing that is not virtue is a suitable possession. Many of these paradoxes were taken over from the Cynics, whose practice in this followed a Socratic tradition.

It might be supposed that the perfectly moral man, being perfectly wise, would never aim at things that in the event he would not succeed in getting or achieving. He would know in advance when the demands of his own nature must be subordinated because they conflicted with the universal plan. He would know when he was fated to fall ill. If he was a general or a statesman he would know what he could undertake with success and what he could not. There are texts which suggest such omniscience. But it was hardly credible that anyone could attain it, however much experience and the art of prophecy might enable him to foresee coming events. Accordingly Seneca declares, as if it were orthodox doctrine, that 'the wise man comes to everything with the proviso "if nothing happens to prevent it"; therefore we say that he succeeds in everything and nothing happens contrary to his expectation, because he presupposes that something can intervene to prevent his design' (*On Services Rendered*, 4.34; cf. Stobaeus 2 p. 115 H.). But there is nothing to show how soon it became orthodox, nor how soon it was appreciated that although no craft, trade, or profession could be correctly carried on except by a wise man, a wise man would not for example be able to play a wind-instrument without learning its technique, and that a wise man could not be expected to learn the techniques of all the arts.

If 'good' is an absolute term, applicable only to moral perfection, if there are no grades of goodness, good men will be very few and far between. Zeno and Cleanthes may have thought goodness a practicable goal; for Chrysippus it had effectively become an unattainable ideal. It became orthodox to recognise that all human beings are, and inevitably remain, bad and unhappy. There was no intermediate state between goodness and badness. Moreover just as 'good' was an absolute, so was 'bad'; there were no grades of badness. This was not a necessary consequence: although it is true that there cannot be grades of perfection—it is an abuse of language to say that one thing is more perfect than another—it does not follow that there are no grades of imperfection. Nevertheless the Stoics maintained that there were no grades of badness: a man, said Chrysippus, who is a cubit below the surface drowns as much as one who is 500 fathoms down. The purpose of this may have been to discourage a man from resting too easily content, from saying to himself 'I'm not so bad' and giving up further effort towards goodness. Yet critics found it absurd that the famous Aristides who became known as 'the Just', should have been as bad and as miserable as the cruel tyrant Phalaris. And although the Stoics defended the paradox, it may be doubted whether they took it very seriously. Perhaps a more effective encouragement to effort was provided by the figure of the man 'making an advance' (*prokoptôn*), still involved in the waters of wickedness, but making his way towards the surface. Critics claimed that he was inconsistent with the paradox, and to common sense he is.

APPROPRIATE ACTIONS

It must frequently happen—perhaps the Stoics thought it was always true—that reason will show that in a particular set of circumstances a certain course of action is appropriate. Such an appropriate action Zeno called *kathêkon,* not a new word, but one which became a technical term in his school. It suggested to him the phrase *kata tinas hêkei,* which may be translated 'it falls to certain persons'. A *kathêkon* is not normally a universal imperative, although later Stoics, at least, recognised *kathêkonta* that admitted no exceptions, arguing that it was always appropriate to act virtuously; this was of no practical importance, since men as they are, not being perfectly good, could not as a matter of fact do anything virtuously. Very many acts are, however, usually appropriate, for example to take care of one's health, or to associate with one's friends. Others are appropriate only in exceptional circumstances, for example to abandon one's property or to commit suicide. But even the act that is usually appropriate still 'falls to certain persons' only; there will be others, however few, for whom it is not appropriate. Whereas to act virtuously is always morally good, and to act faultily always bad, to act appropriately is not in itself either good or bad in the sense of being morally good or bad. It may be appropriate to return a loan, but if the debtor pays in order to establish his credit so that he may obtain a further loan, with which he will abscond, the return will not be a morally good action. If on the other hand he pays with full understanding of why it is right to do so, it is a 'just' and therefore a good action. Accordingly these appropriate actions are called 'intermediate', that is to say they are intermediate between good and bad. Everything depends upon the mental state of the man who performs them. To return a deposit, as Cicero puts it, is appropriate, to do so justly is a correct action. To do so unjustly, he might have added, is a fault. What is externally the same action is ' a correct action' (*katorthôma*) or an 'absolutely appropriate action' if performed by a wise man, an appropriate action if performed by anyone else.

It may be well to enter a caveat here against a mistake which was once common and is still occasionally repeated, that of supposing correct action to be concerned with good things and appropriate action with morally indifferent ones. Misled by a polemical passage in Cicero, probably due to Antiochus (*De Finibus* 4.56), Zeller imagined that Zeno began with correct and incorrect actions aiming respectively at what was good and what was bad, and then 'relaxing his ethical strictness', bridged the gap by introducing 'precedence' among 'indifferent' things and with it the notion of appropriate actions which aimed at what had this inferior sort of value. This makes nonsense of the system. The aim of a thief is not to be wicked but to acquire some money; on the other hand most correct actions must aim at producing some result other than morality and their correctness involves the value of the result. The existence of things with precedence, having their value, to provide an aim is a pre-requisite, whether the action is the virtuous action of the wise man, or the appropriate action of the ordinary man. This value is value for the leading of a natural life. 'What is clearer', says Cicero, 'than that if there was no choosing of the things that accord with nature in preference to those that are against it, all practical wisdom (prudentia) would be at an end?' 'What starting point for appropriate action or material for virtue can I take', asked Chrysippus, 'if I let go of nature and the natural?'

An appropriate action was defined as one which 'when done can be reasonably defended'. It was not necessary that the person who performed it should be able to defend it, as appears from the fact that animals and even plants could act appropriately. Hence appropriate actions are sometimes associated with precepts, by which men of a higher moral standard indicate to their inferiors how they should act. But it is to be noticed that the word 'reasonably' is not necessarily synonymous with 'correctly'. No man is perfectly wise, yet if life is not to be a random affair, there must be rules, certain actions must be recognised as those to be done. It is possible then that a 'reasonable' defence will normally defend what a wise man would defend, but since none but he is infallible, there must remain a chance that it is mistaken. The word was understood in this sense by the sceptic Arcesilaus, who to define a correct action impishly borrowed the Stoic definition of an appropriate action. Since on his principles one could never be sure that any action was correct, but only think it probably correct, he must have taken 'reasonably' in the weak sense of 'correctly so far as can be seen'. Yet it is possible that by the Stoics it was intended to have the strong sense 'by correct reason'. The fact that a man is not perfectly wise does not mean that all the operations of his reason are incorrect. He may not only perform the majority of them correctly but also be aware that they are correct. It is only the sceptic who is never sure that he is right. For the Stoic the correct reasons for defending an action may normally be available, perhaps always available to someone even if not to the man who acts. Clearly the individual may not know why what he does is appropriate for him; there may be differing opinions in the world at large, even among philosophers, about what he ought to do; yet there is something that is appropriate, and that will be defined by correct reason.

We have seen that there is no intermediate state between goodness and badness: all imperfect men are bad men. It was sometimes said that all actions of bad men are faulty, and from this it follows that even when they do what is appropriate, they commit a 'fault'. But there was another way of looking at things, by which the word 'fault' was used in a narrower, but more ordinary, sense of actions which are always such that correct reason will disapprove them, to feel mental pain, to act foolishly, to be frightened, to murder, to steal. Then between these and the actions that are always correct, can be placed those that are appropriate or inappropriate according to circumstances, but not in themselves morally good or bad. The appropriate are exemplified by such things as honouring one's parents, associating with friends, getting married, going for a walk (Diogenes Laertius 7.108–9); some of these will almost always be the right thing to do, others only occasionally. One could draw up a similar list of inappropriate acts. It is important that it is individual actions of this kind that are appropriate; when it is said for example that marriage is appropriate, that does not mean that it is appropriate for all men in all circumstances, but that it will be appropriate for most individual men.

The appropriate action should always be preferred, and so the ordinary man, who has not attained wisdom, can still attempt to choose the actions that are appropriate to himself. If as time goes on he makes fewer and fewer mistakes, he is said to be 'making progress' (he is *prokoptôn*), that is he is progressing towards emerging from his folly. Finally he may be imagined as always making the right choice; now the only difference between him and the wise man is that the reasoning that leads him is not perfect, it cannot be relied on always to reach the right conclusion. Chrysippus drew the conclusion that, not being wise, the man who had taken all but the last step on the road of progress must still be a fool, a bad man, and an unhappy man. His appropriate actions must still be faulty in that they are not dictated by perfect reason. To ancient critics this position, logical though it was on the premise that good and bad, wise and foolish, are absolute terms that do not admit of degrees, seemed absurdly paradoxical, as was also the further claim that the change from folly to wisdom would be so infinitesimal that it would not be noticed at the instant it took place.

There is little evidence that later Stoics, from the time of Panaetius onwards, paid attention to the extreme position that an appropriate action was still a faulty action if performed by a man who was not wise. Rather they seem to have supposed that the individual action performed by an ordinary man was neither good nor bad, whereas strictly speaking what was morally indifferent was the content of the action, not the mental processes that went with it.

Suicide

Among actions occasionally appropriate was suicide. The justification for living or for dying was to be found not in the happiness or misery arising from one's moral state but in the presence of advantages, that is of what accords with man's nature in the narrow sense of that word (see p. 32 above). 'A man', says Cicero's Stoic (*De Finibus* 3.60), 'in whom there predominates what accords with nature, has the duty of remaining in life, one in whom what is contrary to nature predominates or seems about to predominate has the duty of departing from life: from this it is clear that it is sometimes the duty of a wise man to depart from life, although he is happy, and of the foolish man to remain in life, although he is wretched'. How man is to strike the balance between factors for living or dying is not obvious, since it cannot be done by the mere enumeration of advantages and disadvantages; they must be assigned values and weighed against one another. But a wise man, it may be supposed, will be capable of this calculation; he will know when the disabilities of disease or old age grow to outweigh such natural advantages, e.g. the possession of sight or of children, as he may still enjoy.

It is also clear, I think, that the man who is not wise will sometimes miscalculate, committing suicide when to go on living would be appropriate, and maintaining life when it would be appropriate to die. But the unwise do not always miscalculate or always fail to perform appropriate actions; and so they will sometimes kill themselves when they should, even although they may more often cling to life when they should not. The fact that they sometimes fail to recognise what is appropriate is no reason for supposing that suicide is never appropriate for them.[1]

[1]In his interesting chapter on suicide J. M. Rist, *Stoic Philosophy* 233ff., rather hesitantly suggests that Chrysippus believed suicide to be inappropriate for an unwise man, unless perhaps he received a divine sign. He thinks that this was also the view of Zeno, about whom there was a story that one day he tripped and broke his toe, struck the ground and exclaimed, from an unidentified tragedian's *Niobe*, 'I am coming; why do you call me?' and killed himself. The anecdote is probably worthless, and even if it is true, the breaking of the toe may have been the last straw in the sum of disabilities rather than a divine sign. Rist quotes a phrase of Chrysippus from a passage preserved by Plutarch *Moralia* 1039 D, 'and it is appropriate for bad men to remain alive'. But this is in a sentence which is Plutarch's summary, and it is unnecessary to suppose Chrysippus to have meant that it was always appropriate; the context suggests his point to have been that wickedness is no reason for suicide.

If a wise man suffering from a painful terminal disease would be right to kill himself, it would seem absurd that a sufferer who had not attained perfect wisdom should be wrong to do so.

According to some Stoics a man could also appropriately kill himself for the sake of his country or his friends (Diogenes Laertius 7.130). Here we get away from the idea that suicide is dependent on one's own balance of natural advantage. It will still be concerned with such advantages, but now with obtaining them or preserving them for other people. Another text (Cramer, *Paris Anecdota* 4.403) says that the Stoics recognised five reasons for leaving life's banquet, corresponding to five reasons for breaking up a real party: a great advantage, as when the oracle commanded a man to kill himself for his country, the irruption of autocrats who try to force men to shameful actions, protracted disease, poverty, and madness. Here there is to be seen a third type of reasonable cause for suicide, that of avoiding the commission of immoral acts. This would seem contrary to the position of Chrysippus, whom Plutarch represents as thinking that the standard for living or suicide was not to be found in things good or bad but in the 'intermediate' natural advantages (*Moralia* 1042 D). Elsewhere he says that the Stoics maintained that it would have been appropriate for Heraclitus and Pherecydes to lose their virtue and wisdom, if they had thereby been able to escape their dropsy and consumption by lice (*Moralia* 1064 A). Whether this was the opinion of Chrysippus or of some follower, it clearly drives to an extreme the principle that one's morality or immorality should have no weight in the decision whether to live or die.

The topic of suicide constantly recurs among the Roman Stoics. Seneca glorifies it as the road to freedom. It has been said that he was in love with death. Certainly fascinated by it, he exults in the thought that it is not hard to find; there is always a way open. 'The eternal law has done nothing better than its gift to us of one entry to life, and many ways out . . . there is one thing in life of which we need not complain : it detains no one' (*Letters* 70.14). 'In any kind of slavery we shall show that there is a way to freedom. If through its own faults the mind is sick and wretched, a man may end his miseries and himself. . . . Wherever you look there is an end to your ills. Do you see that precipice? Down there is the way to freedom. Do you see that sea, that river, that well? Freedom sits there below. Do you see that little withered, barren tree? Freedom hangs from its branches. Do you see your throat, your gullet, your heart? They are ways of escape from servitude' (*On Anger* 3.15). The context of this latter passage is the cruelties of tyrannical masters, but Seneca thinks of escaping not only these but also one's own imperfections. That is unusual. Elsewhere he mentions as justification for suicide mainly what is morally indifferent, lack of necessities, the infirmity of age, incurable disease, the threat of torture. For all his glorification of death and his praise of the freedom it brings, not a freedom to do anything but an absence of the constraints of life, at other times his belief that it is not to be feared suggests that it should be calmly awaited. 'A man is on his way to kill you. Wait for him. Why should you anticipate him? Why undertake to execute another man's cruelty? Do you envy your hangmen his task or would you spare him from it?' (*Letters* 70.8).

Epictetus often uses phrases like 'The door stands open'. Sometimes it is not clear whether he means 'You can kill yourself' or 'A natural death will supervene', but there are several passages (e.g. *Discourses* II.1.19) where suicide is clearly intended. But his thought seems to be that certain death may properly be hastened, rather than that one should be ready to find death preferable to life. It is a man's duty to bear the pains that God sends him: only if deprived of life's necessities does he know that God is sounding the recall. He imagined himself approached by young pupils saying 'Epictetus, we can no longer endure being prisoners along with our wretched body, feeding it and giving it drink and putting it to sleep and cleaning it, and then through it associating with these men here and those men there. Are not these things indifferent and no concern of ours? Is not death no evil? Are we not God's kinsmen and have we not come thence? Let us depart to the place whence we have come, let us be freed at last from these fetters that hang heavy upon us.' And he would reply, 'Men, wait for God. When he gives the signal and relieves you of this service then depart to Him; but for the present endure to inhabit this place where he has stationed you'. (*Discourses* I.9. 12–16.)

Marcus Aurelius reflected that with advancing years the

mind's understanding might decay; the man may still breathe and feed, have perception and appetite, but no longer see accurately where his duty lies nor judge clearly whether the time has come to usher himself out of life (3.1). He does not here state explicitly what should be the reasons for an ageing man's suicide. Elsewhere he once quotes Epictetus' simile according to which one would leave a room if it became too full of smoke (5.29), and Epictetus had, it seems, thought primarily of bodily pains and handicaps. But in several places he shows the feeling that the only life that is worth living is a moral life. By that he does not mean the life of the ideal Stoic sage, a dream in which he has no interest, but one informed by kindliness and devoid of passions. If you cannot escape from your vices, you should die, performing thereby one good action at least (9.2; 10.8. 1–2). 'Who prevents you from being good and simple? Just resolve to live no longer if you are not such. Reason does not demand that you should live if you lack these qualities' (10.32). The uppermost motive in such reflections may be to exhort himself to effort, but behind them lies the thought that a confirmed sinner would rightly consider himself unfit to live. In another passage he thinks of circumstances where something stronger than he prevents him from achieving a sound purpose; then should life not be worth living if the purpose is not achieved, one should leave it cheerfully and with kindly feelings towards the obstacle that intervened (8.47). Something of this sort may have been in his mind when he wrote to the Senate after the discovery of Cassius' conspiracy that he wished none of the accomplices to be executed and that if he could not secure this he would hasten his own death (Dio Cassius 71.30). Here is a third reason for suicide, and one no more orthodox than that of failure to cast off vice. It was basic to Stoicism that intention was everything and achievement nothing. Marcus could not escape the normal human feeling that unless he could execute his purpose he would be a failure.

THE GOAL OF LIFE

By Zeno's time a philosopher might expect to be asked what he held to be the 'end' (*telos*) of life. This word combined the meanings of 'goal' and of 'perfection'. The 'end' is at once that towards which all one's efforts should be directed and also the supreme good. It was assumed that a man's activities should be so integrated and subordinated to a single end : Aristotle takes it for granted at *Nicomachean Ethics* 1095a 15ff.; the 'democratic' man, whom Plato ridicules in the Republic, with his shifting interests, each allowed its turn, had no support among philosophers.

During the first two centuries of the Stoic school successive leaders used different formulas to express the end of life. It is disputed whether these changes reflected alterations of doctrine or attempts to define one and the same ideal more accurately. The ideal was that of 'living consistently' or of 'living consistently with nature'; each phrase is often said to be the Stoic description of the goal. Did the various philosophers find substantially different meanings in their formulas or, to use the language of Arius Didymus, was their concern merely to 'give them further articulation' (Stobaeus 2.7.6a)? I believe the latter alternative to be nearer the truth.

The problem resolves itself into asking what interpretation was put on the phrase 'consistently with nature'. Is the right life one that accords with what is specifically human nature or one that falls in with the purposes of the universe? Or can the two aims be combined? If so, how? Did the different heads of the school differ in their answers to these questions?

It is not certain that the wording 'to live consistently with nature' originated with Zeno. Diogenes Laertius reports that in his book *On Man's Nature* he said (and was the first to say) that the end was 'to live consistently with nature' (7.87). This definition is ascribed to him by several other authors. But Arius Didymus has a different story:

Zeno expressed the end as follows : 'to live consistently', that is to live by one harmonious plan (*logos*), as those who live in conflict are unhappy. His successors gave this further articulation and produced the phrase 'to live consistently with nature'; they took it that Zeno's expression was an incomplete statement. Cleanthes, who took over the school from him, was the first to add 'with nature'—Chrysippus, wishing to make the definition clearer, expressed it in this way, 'to live according to experience of what happens by nature.'

It is hard to put this aside; many guess that Chrysippus interpreted Zeno's language in the book *On Man's Nature* to show that he would have been ready to accept the later formula, which added the words 'with nature', and they may be right. But even so, is it justifiable to look for a difference of substance as well as of language? Posidonius was later to say that Chrysippus' definition was equivalent to 'living consistently' (Galen, *On the Views of Hippocrates and Plato* p. 450 M); in other words he saw no essential difference between him and Zeno. In this I believe him to have been correct. To 'live consistently' is an inadequate phrase to express Zeno's ideal of how to live. One man might direct the whole of his activities consistently towards making money or another towards writing the longest epic poem the world had known: it would be consistent for the latter to neglect his parents, if he could do so safely, and to provide for his needs by some single undetectable fraud rather than protracted honest labour. Zeno must have meant the single plan by which life should be lived to be a plan formed by correct reason, and this will be one that is natural, in the sense that it accords both with man's nature and with universal nature. No one in antiquity suggested that there was any real difference between Zeno and Chrysippus in their views of the 'end': that has been left to modern historians, who welcome conflicts as grist to their mills.

Cleanthes is said to have interpreted 'living consistently with nature' to mean 'consistently with universal nature', whereas Chrysippus understood 'both universal nature and in particular human nature' (Diogenes Laertius 7.89). It may be doubted whether there was any real difference in theory. The distinction between human and universal nature can be reconciled. When what normally accords with human nature is in conflict with the dispositions of universal nature, a rational man sees that the latter have precedence, and so it is then natural for him, as the rational being that man properly is, to follow universal nature, abandoning his normal preferences. On the other hand, these normal human preferences are usually acceptable to reason, and in accord with universal nature. Hence an opposition between human nature and universal nature is illusory. Chrysippus cannot have intended to tamper with the ideal of life in accord with universal nature; he was adding that such a life was also consistent with human nature. Nor did he intend his formula, 'by experience of what happens by nature', to differ from the traditional 'consistently with nature'. He meant that consistency with nature could be obtained only through observation of nature's ways.

Chrysippus' successors invented new formulas which had a family likeness. The passage of Arius continues as follows:

> Diogenes (of Babylon): 'to calculate well in the selection of things that accord with nature and in their non-selection'; Archedemus: 'to live performing all actions appropriate to one'; Antipater: 'to live selecting what is in accord with nature and not selecting what is against nature', and he often put it like this too, 'to do everything that lies within oneself, perpetually and infallibly, to get what by nature takes the lead'.[1]

Another source ascribes to Archedemus the formula 'to live selecting the greatest and most important things that accord with nature, being unable to overlook them'. This, which is in no way inconsistent with what is ascribed to him by Arius, brings him into line with Antipater, who was probably his senior.

These formulas were not intended to replace that of 'living consistently with nature' but to make it more precise. They insist that consistency with nature does not mean having what is natural, but wanting it. Diogenes by introducing the mention of selection emphasised the means through which the harmony with nature was to be achieved, a continued correct solving of the problems offered by life. Although Chrysippus had not included selection in his definition, he was well aware of its importance.[2] None of the formulas are necessarily to be understood to restrict the 'things that accord with nature' to what accords with man's nature in a narrow sense. As has previously been emphasised, man's rationality makes him see as natural

---

[1]The word *proēgoumenon*, translated 'what takes the lead', may mean either 'what is important' or 'what initiates, gives a lead'. Antipater may have thought that what is natural beckons a man on, as it were.

[2]Epictetus, *Discourses* 2.6.9, Cicero, *De Finibus* 3.31.

the promotion of the interests of his fellow-men and the acceptance of 'misfortunes' that Providence may impose on him in the execution of its wider purposes. This is essential to the Stoic philosophy, and it seems most improbable that it was overlooked by these members of the school.

Nevertheless there is some evidence which has been taken to show that they did overlook it. Plutarch states the Stoic goal of life to be 'the well-calculated selection and acceptance of the primary natural things and to do all that lies with oneself to get the primary natural things' (*Moralia* 1071 A). The 'primary natural things', although nowhere enumerated, must be a restricted class, not identical with what is seen as natural by developed reason. One might suspect that the word 'primary' had been unfairly introduced for polemical purposes by Carneades, and that Plutarch was following him; Carneades had maintained that the goal of life must be one of nine things; it could be either to aim at pleasure or absence of pain or the primary natural things, or to secure one of these objectives, or to secure one of these objectives *plus* what is noble and fine. But Posidonius wrote of some unnamed Stoics that they 'reduce living consistently to doing all that is possible for the sake of the primary natural things'; he added that the Chrysippean formula of 'living by experience of what happens by nature' was a correct interpretation of 'living consistently', a phrase that had been 'shabbily' taken to mean getting what is morally indifferent'. Yet he was here engaged in polemic and perhaps therefore in misrepresentation:[1] surely no Stoic can have supposed the *summum bonum* to be the *getting* of what was morally indifferent. Posidonius may have intended not to elucidate Antipater's meaning, but to show what interpretation could be put on his formula. If that is so, to restrict choice to the primary natural things was a misrepresentation.

Diogenes then did not make any fundamental change by calling the end or supreme good well-calculated choice and rejection of what is natural. It will not always be possible to have everything that is natural; for example health, wealth, and

[1] It is noteworthy that he said in this context that working for the sake of the primary natural things was on a par with working for pleasure or for absence of disturbance, i.e. he was operating with the Carneadean division of goals in life.

falling in with God's purposes are all natural, but one may have to choose between health and wealth, or between health and willing acceptance of a sickness that is part of the divine plan. In the latter case it is impossible to be healthy, but an imperfect man might 'choose' health in the sense that he would wish to keep his health instead of rationally accepting his illness. But this new formula was open to an objection: a well-calculated choice must be made with some end in view. Carneades seems to have argued that the end towards which one's actions are directed must be one's end in life; so the well-calculated choice must be choice of what serves a well-calculated choice and so on *ad infinitum*. Antipater's modifications appear to be designed to meet this criticism. The formula 'to live selecting what is in accord with nature and not selecting what is against nature' avoids the questions 'With what aim do you select some natural things and reject others? Why is one selection well-calculated?' The new formula does not invite these questions, for it may seem self-evident that the natural should be chosen and the unnatural rejected. 'Natural' must now be understood to mean what accords with universal nature, although this will of course very frequently also be what accords with restricted human nature.[1]

Antipater's second formula is intended to meet another objection raised by Carneades. Even if *selection* of the natural is virtuous and to be included in the supreme good, the natural cannot be deprived of value, and its *possession* ought to be part of that good, part of one's aim. Antipater introduced 'getting of the natural' into his formula, but held to the orthodox belief that it formed no part of the supreme good. He made use of an analogy with an archer, who tries to hit a target, but whose aim is to be a good archer. He will achieve that aim if he always discharges his arrow correctly, and his achievement is not lessened if something outside his control causes it to miss the target; one might illustrate Antipater's meaning by instancing the flight of a bird across the trajectory or the collapse of the target. This formula, then, which by including the natural

[1]Some writers would not accept this, believing that the formula is equivalent to that of Diogenes, and must have been used by Antipater before he tried to meet Carneades' criticism.

objectives recognises that they are essential for moral action, also establishes their relation to it; not their acquisition, but the attempt to acquire them constitutes morality.

But the goal of selecting 'what accords with nature' is an uninspiring one, if it is considered what these things are. They are all morally indifferent things, e.g. health, wealth, or comfort. When reason extends a man's conception of nature so that he finds it natural to care for others beside himself, it is their health, wealth and comfort that he will choose. Even when his reason falls in with the universal reason that rules the world, he will still be selecting what is morally indifferent, e.g. sickness, exile, and death. But such acceptance of what conflicts with what is usually natural must be a rare event, and so the formulas we have been discussing will be easily understood as identifying 'what accords with nature' with 'what has precedence'.[1] Among these a large place is taken by the 'primary natural things', so that Posidonius, even though inaccurate, may have been loosely speaking justified in complaining that these Stoics reduced their goal to trying to get such things, and that although this avoided the criticisms of the Sophists (by which he seems to have meant the Academics), it was a shabby interpretation of 'living consistently with nature'. Essentially the supreme good is harmony with universal nature, and the attempt to get what is in the narrow sense natural for man is merely incidental to that aim.[2]

Panaetius' formula, 'to live according to the starting-points given us by nature' (p. 126), was a novelty in its wording rather than its content. Cicero seems to be following him when he writes 'we should act so as not to strive in any way against universal nature but while keeping to that follow our own nature' (*On Duties* 1.110). That is exactly the doctrine we have found in Chrysippus. It is consistent with Panaetius' formula, because reason is one of man's starting-points, in fact the one that distinguishes him from the beasts (cf. Cicero, *On Duties* 1.11-14), and reason must show the desirability of living in harmony with universal nature. The formula's effect is not to

[1]See p. 29.

[2]For Posidonius' own explanation of 'living consistently with nature' see p. 137.

change the goal, but to insist upon the fact that it is one towards which man's own nature directs him.

It has been argued in the preceding pages that to live consistently with nature was an aim accepted by all Stoics, that this nature was universal nature, with which man's fully-developed nature must always coincide, and which in great part allowed him to have what suited his own individual nature. But this life consistent with nature is also internally self-consistent, and there are passages in which this is stressed. Thus Zeno is said to have identified 'living consistently' with 'living according to a single harmonious plan', and happiness, which was another way of referring to the goal, was described by him, Cleanthes, and Chrysippus as 'an easy flow of life', that is to say the current of life was to be regular and undisturbed. Panaetius, as reported by Cicero, remarked that whereas other animals have very limited powers of memory and foresight, man can understand cause and effect and by the use of analogy see the whole course of his life and prepare for it. Elsewhere he spoke of the importance of uniformity (*aequabilitas*) in the whole of one's life, to be attained only by keeping within one's own capacities (Cicero, *On Duties* 1.111). This consistency and absence of conflict is an essential part of happiness, but only to be had through accord with the divine reason that rules all the world.

THE PASSIONS

It is sometimes said that the Stoics wished to eradicate the emotions; and this, it is argued, is as undesirable as it is impracticable, for without emotion man would lose the mainspring of action.

> Ils ôtent à nos cœurs le principal ressort;
> Ils font cesser de vivre avant que l'on soit mort[1]
> > (De la Fontaine, *Fables* 12.20).

This criticism is at best a half-truth. What the Stoics wished to abolish was not emotion but 'passion' (*pathos*) or, as Cicero translated the word, 'mental disturbance'. They had no word

[1] They take the mainspring from our heart; they make us stop living before we are dead.

that corresponds to the English 'emotion'. This may mean that they underestimated emotion's importance; it does not imply that they wanted to get rid of it. It is, however, true that they did not adequately recognise the autonomous origin of emotions, but tried too much to treat them as the outcome of intellectual forces.

The love of parents for children is an emotion. It was regarded by the Stoics as natural and proper. They pointed out that it was to be seen in brute animals, where there is no question of its arising from calculation. Some animals have a social instinct: in men this is developed so that they have feelings of friendship towards their fellows. These too are emotions, and result in altruistic actions. A particular form is love, defined as 'a design to make friends, due to visible beauty'. This is an intellectualist description, but we should call what is described an emotion. All these psychological states are perfectly acceptable. Marcus Aurelius recalls that one of the lessons taught him by Sextus was to be entirely passionless yet full of affection. The objectionable 'passion' is something different, and can be understood only by following the Stoic theory of appetition, which may be set out as follows:

All animals are impelled to action by a movement in their *psychê*[1] called a *hormê*, 'impulse' or 'drive'. In a brute beast this follows directly upon the stimulus of a presentation[2] (to invent an instance, a dog that scents a hare immediately wants to chase it). But in a human being the impulse does not exist without a mental act of assent. (A man who sees a hare does not immediately desire to chase it: he must first entertain and assent to the presentation 'that hare is something to be chased'.) The sharp distinction between man and other animals cannot be accepted today, but to the Stoics this human peculiarity was important because it allowed man to be treated as an agent responsible for all his actions. But the impulse in man's *psyche* may get out of hand; it may become excessive; the movement of the *psyche* becomes unreasonable and unnatural. It is then a 'passion', a disturbance, of which there are four generic kinds:

---

[1] A mixture of air and fire, responsible for all the functions of the living animal; see below p. 82.

[2] See below p. 85.

fear, lust,[1] mental pain, and mental pleasure. These are disobedient to reason: Chrysippus used as a simile a comparison
between a man walking and one running; the former can halt
instantly, the latter cannot. Similarly the man in whom impulse
is excessive cannot immediately check it; anger and fear cannot
be voluntarily arrested in a moment. Now since a passion is by
definition excessive, it should if possible be avoided or prevented or, if ever entertained, suppressed. A perfect man will
not suffer from any of these disturbances.

Let us next examine the four kinds of passion. Fear is a contraction of the *psyche* caused by the belief that something bad
is impending. This contraction must be understood literally:
it causes the physical effects of fear, paleness, shivering, thump-
ing of the heart. But the belief is false: what is feared is not
what a Stoic calls 'bad', but one of the morally indifferent
things, e.g. death, pain, ill-repute. Fear is the result of exaggerating their importance, of believing that they will bring real
harm, whereas they do not touch man's essential moral being,
and if they come are to be accepted as part of the great plan of
nature. Lust is a longing for something believed to be good, but
again falsely so believed, since the supposed good is morally
indifferent; in physical terms it is described as an expansion
of the *psyche*. A great many species of lust were distinguished,
among which anger rather unexpectedly appears, defined as
lust for revenge on someone who seems to have done us wrong.
Mental pain is a contraction of the *psyche* resulting from the
belief, again erroneous, that something bad is present. Among
its species are envy, jealousy, grief and, more surprisingly, pity.
The condemnation of pity has been bad for the Stoics' reputation. But it was logical if pity is understood as arising from the
belief that what the other person suffers is really bad. If sorrow
or resentment are not to be felt at one's own sufferings, why
should they be felt for those of another? Even those who

[1] I use the word 'lust' in a wide sense, to represent *epithymia*, which
is often translated 'desire'. But 'desire' is inadequate to express the
meaning of the Greek word, which suggests 'yearning after a thing',
setting one's heart on it. The attitude towards it of the Platonists
had been ambivalent: although it was for them a necessary part of
the human person it was also regrettable and needed firm discipline
by reason.

cannot accept this analysis of pity must admit that it can be a feeling that disturbs a man to no good purpose and distorts his judgment; in such cases it is to be recognised as what was meant by a 'passion', and must be regarded, at least by a Stoic, as something to be suppressed.

Finally pleasure, a word which like '*epithymia*' had kept bad company in earlier thought, was defined as an irrational expansion of the *psyche* caused by the supposed presence of something good. Again the nature of the thing over which pleasure is felt is, in Stoic eyes, misjudged. What is thought to be good is not in fact good, but at the best, 'acceptable'. It is important to recognise that the passion called pleasure is essentially a mental phenomenon and does not belong to the body. Its species include pleasure at unexpected 'benefits', pleasure at other people's misfortunes, pleasure caused by deceit or magic. It is to be distinguished from what may be called agreeable physical feelings; these also have the same name of pleasure. The danger of confusion is increased by the fact that there are 'passionate' mental pleasures closely associated with sensual physical pleasures. If the pleasantness of experience of touch, sight, taste, smell and hearing was thought to be good and important, a pleasure arose that was passionate and to be censured (Cicero, *Talks at Tusculum* 4.20), but the agreeable feelings themselves were not condemned by any Stoic, although there was no agreement on their exact status. Cleanthes denied that they were 'in accord with nature' or had any value in life, Archedemus thought that they were natural but without value, like the hairs in the armpit, while Panaetius believed some to be natural and others not.

The general denial of value to physical pleasure was apparently due to two factors, the first hostility to Epicureanism, the other the observation that it was an influence that easily corrupted the man who experienced it. If one attaches any value to pleasure, one is tempted to attach too much. Hence although Cleanthes' position seems untenable, for physical pleasure often supervenes automatically when we have things that are natural for us, it was not obviously wrong to hold that we should aim at those things purely for their own sake and not because they bring pleasure. Such pleasure was not something to which any weight should be attached; on the other hand it was not to be rejected. But the pleasure which is a passion and condemnable is something different; it is in Stoic eyes the result of a faulty judgment. Often this will be a judgment that pleasure in the other sense is in fact something good. This causes a mental disturbance: the pleasure that is a passion will cause the subject to direct his energies to obtaining or keeping the agreeable feelings towards which he should be indifferent.

Passions, which are to be seen as particular instances of disturbance resting on individual faulty judgments, are related to more permanent states. On the one hand some people have a proclivity to some particular passion or passions : an irascible man has a proclivity to anger. On the other hand repeated indulgence in a passion leads to a diseased state of mind, in which there is a permanent and generalised false opinion : for example greed repeatedly indulged will breed avarice, or a belief that all monetary gain is very desirable. Chrysippus developed this line of thought by drawing parallels between the body and the *psyche*. Some persons have a tendency to certain illnesses, and certain physical disturbances establish chronic sickness. Cicero found these similes unnecessary (*Talks at Tusculum* 4.23), but they were apt for one who thought the *psyche* to be as material as the body, and they call attention to some undoubted psychological facts. They also are the basis of what was to become a popular metaphor : the philosopher is the physician of the soul. Understanding the nature of the disease, he is best able to prescribe methods for avoiding or curing it.

For later Stoics the practical task of suppressing the passions loomed large, and often absorbed more of their energies than thinking about the basic theory of their system. The treatment of passions as diseases confirmed the ideal of their complete elimination. This aim of being without passions (*apatheia*) was contrasted with the ideal of moderation in passion (*metriopatheia*) adopted by Peripatetics in dependence on Aristotle, who had held that it was wrong to feel either too little or too much fear, anger, or other emotion. The distinction, although justified, can be exaggerated. The Stoic passion is an excessive uncontrolled drive, due to an overestimation of indifferent things, but there is also a correct drive towards these same things. The moderate passion of the Peripatetic is a correct feeling, and so could perhaps not be regarded by a Stoic as a passion at all.

But members of the two schools would be likely to differ over what was correct. What a Peripatetic would regard as a correct amount of anger or of fear would seem excessive to a Stoic.

These were the views on the passions that were generally agreed among the Stoics. We must go on to consider some differences and difficulties. In the first place, a passion is 'an excessive impulse (or drive)' and the exact nature of what was meant by the word *hormê* (impulse or drive) is not easy to grasp. In children and animals it must be seen simply as a desire to do something, which will unless hindered be followed by movements in the *psyche* that will effect bodily action. In an adult, however, it is associated with an act of assent and a judgment. According to Galen, whose view is accepted by many modern scholars, Zeno believed that the impulse which was a passion supervened on the judgment. Psychic expansion and contraction are plausibly seen as different from the judgments that cause them, and some think that Zeno took them to be the movements of an irrational element in the *psyche*. Chrysippus, on the other hand, identified the impulse with a *logos* that commands a man to act, or a judgment. Later Stoics followed him when they defined it as 'a movement of thought towards something in the field of action'.

The contrast between the two accounts is clear, yet Chrysippus himself does not seem to have emphasised it. He retained Zeno's language, according to which a passion was 'an excessive impulse and disobedient to reason' and specifically interpreted the last words to mean, not 'the product of perverted reason' but 'not moved by reason at all', 'having abandoned reason'. Moreover Plutarch and Galen quoted from Chrysippus some passages which imply either that passion succeeds a judgment or that it opposes one; perhaps these were either carelessly written or belong to a time before he had adopted his final position, which was that the impulse was not to be distinguished from the judgment. He defined mental pain as 'a fresh belief in the presence of something bad', fear as 'expectation of something bad', and so on. On the other hand this view seems to have been anticipated by Zeno, to whom Posidonius ascribed a definition of mental pain as 'a fresh opinion that something bad for oneself is present'. Elsewhere this is represented as Chrysippean doctrine, but it is improbable that

Posidonius was mistaken in his ascription, since Cicero says that it was Zeno who added the word 'fresh', so rightly altering an earlier form of the definition (*Talks at Tusculum* 3.75).

A possible solution is that, seeing a complex which comprised an opinion and a necessarily connected psychic movement, Zeno did not clearly identify passion with either element, but regarded it sometimes as the one, sometimes as the other. When, however, he said that the impulse of a passion is disobedient to reason, the phrase could suggest that the *psyche* contained two elements, a rational one and another that was irrational and insubordinate. Cleanthes perhaps understood the doctrine in this way, if a dialogue in verse between Calculation and Anger may be taken literally.

Calculation:	Whatever is it that you want? Explain.
Anger:	I want? I want to do whatever I want.
Calculation:	A regal wish! But say it once again.
Anger:	Whatever I desire I want to happen.

The lines were, however, quoted by Posidonius in order to claim the support of Cleanthes for his own view that the *psyche* had both rational and irrational powers. He may have misinterpreted them for this purpose. By Anger Cleanthes may have meant not an irrational force but perverted reason, here presented in an imaginary dialogue with (true) Calculation.[1] Chrysippus then decided that the passion must be identified with the opinion that was involved with it. This seems an odd doctrine. That a passion is something that supervenes on a judgment or belief might be argued: it hardly seems to be the judgment itself. Chrysippus seems to have been led to this improbable view through believing that in adult man the command-centre was essentially rational. He could not admit the existence outside it of any other autonomous force. Hence it was necessary that a passion should be an act of reason, or an intellectual act, although a perverted one. This had the advantage of appearing to show that it would not be a complicated matter to get rid of the passions: all that would be needed is

[1]It is possible that Cleanthes did not use the word *thymos* as Stoics usually did, of a kind of anger, but in a wider meaning which covers desire in general.

the firm belief that morally indifferent things are neither good nor bad.

But although Chrysippus did not recognise an independent irrational force, he did admit that the passion had irrational effects. Probably he sometimes explained mental pain more fully as 'a fresh belief in the presence of something bad, by reason of which men think they ought to suffer contraction' (of the *psyche*). Certainly he spoke of pleasure as 'a swelling' or 'elation'. It may perhaps be supposed that these contractions and elations correspond to the feelings with which we are inclined to identify the passions. Chrysippus' point is that they are not autonomous forces but the intended result of faulty judgments; it is better to give the name 'passion' to what is essential and primary in this complex.

The Chrysippean view is open to some obvious objections, which were seen and in a measure answered. First there is the experience of being the victim of a passion and of fighting it, of being afraid and knowing that one ought not to be afraid. How can one simultaneously believe that something bad is threatening and that what is threatening is not bad? Some Stoics seem to have explained this by saying that the two beliefs were held alternately in such rapid succession that both appeared to be held continuously (Plutarch, *Moralia* 446 f). Secondly, animals and children, not being rational, cannot suffer from passions; yet they appear to be afraid, pained, etc. It was argued that children have only something analogous to passions: they are so volatile in changing from tears to laughter, from apparent fright to happy play, that they cannot be genuinely wretched or frightened. Thirdly, why if passions are judgments do they vary in intensity? Why do they frequently abate? Does the judgment change? Chrysippus saw the difficulty and answered that the judgment, e.g. that something bad is present, does not change, but that as time passes the contraction of the *psyche* is relaxed, and probably also the impulse to contract. That, it would seem, is to say that the thought 'my *psyche* ought to contract', which accompanied the judgment that something bad was present, becomes less insistent. Alternatively, the impulse remains the same but its effects are blocked 'through some supervening condition'. Galen complains that Chrysippus did not explain further the mechanism he had in mind. One can only guess. The word used for 'condition' (*diathesis*) is elsewhere used, perhaps only used, of lasting conditions of the *psyche*. Possibly these intervene to restore the status quo after an initial disturbance. Chrysippus compared the way in which we cease to weep or to laugh, the causes of tears and laughter becoming less effective as time goes on.

THE GOOD EMOTIONS

There are correct impulses as well as excessive ones. At some time these were given the name *eupatheiai*, 'good emotions'. Cicero calls them *constantiae*, perhaps 'steady states', as opposed to the uncontrolled exaggerated drive of the passion.[1] Alongside desire there is wish or well-reasoned appetite, alongside fear there is caution or well-reasoned avoidance, alongside pleasure there is joy or well-reasoned elation. But these states of feeling were confined to the wise man, who alone had correct reason. That is why there is no correct impulse of mental pain. The wise man must accept all that happens to him as providentially ordered, and there is nothing morally bad in him which might provide a rational cause for distress.

But here a problem presents itself. Were these good emotions related to what was truly good and bad or, like the passions, to what was morally indifferent? Andronicus, who at the end of the first century BC listed Stoic definitions of virtues and vices, passions and good emotions, explained two kinds of joy as due to the presence of truly good things and caution as the avoidance of immoral acts. Seneca defined joy as the mental elation of a man who trusts in his own goods and truths, and insisted that these were things that could not be taken from him (*Letter* 59). If joy is a thing of this kind, it is intelligible that it at least should preserve the wise. Other authors write as if the good emotions were identifiable with correct impulses towards or from morally indifferent objects, whereas excessive impulses constituted the passions (Plutarch *Moralia* 449a, Cicero, *Talks at Tusculum* 4.12-14, Lactantius *Div. Inst.* 6.15). But if this is right, it is hard to see why they should be confined to the wise. The ordinary man does not

---

[1]Can he have misread *eupatheia* as *eustatheia*, 'stability'?

always suffer a passion when he might do so : the same danger may frighten one man and not another. Although the latter's reason may not be perfect, it may function correctly sometimes and so produce a correct impulse. Accordingly one should perhaps conclude that these authors misunderstood or misrepresented the Stoic view. Yet it must be admitted that even the assumption that good emotions were concerned with what was really good or bad leaves the wise man's monopoly of well-reasoned appetite and caution somewhat surprising. Why should not an imperfect man altruistically wish other men's moral good, and desire to avoid committing a crime himself? Perhaps it was thought that in such cases his drive was necessarily inadequate, and that his emotion could not therefore be well-reasoned.

CONCLUSION

This analytical and sometimes adverse account of Stoic ethics must appear somewhat arid and may fail to give an adequate picture of their attraction. If certain assumptions are accepted, the whole system hangs together and so can claim intellectual respectability. It recognises as legitimate objects of endeavour much to which men automatically attach value, but in the last resort things which they cannot control are of no importance. Happiness depends on what is entirely a man's own doing, the operation of his mind: if he judges correctly and holds steadfastly to truth he will be a perfect being, whom misfortune may strike but will never harm.

> The wise man will be more rightly called a king than was Tarquin, who could rule neither himself nor his people . . . more rightly rich than Crassus . . . All things will rightly be called his, for he alone knows how to use them; rightly too will he be called beautiful, for the features of the mind are more beautiful than those of the body, rightly the only free man, since he obeys no master and is the servant of no greed, rightly invincible, for though his body may be bound, no fetters can be put on his mind . . . If it is true that none but the wise are good and all the good are blessed, is anything more to be studied than philosophy or anything more divine than virtue? (Cicero, *De Finibus* 3.75–6.)

4

The System: Natural Science

For the Greeks 'physics' was the study of the physical world and its changes. It was therefore a wider subject than modern physics. For the Stoics it included psychology and epistemology, for these deal with activities of the *psyche,* which they held to be a material entity. These subjects we readily accept as the concern of philosophers, but explanation of the physical world we leave to the scientists. Among the Greeks things were otherwise, and for the Stoics cosmology was an integral part of philosophy, and inextricably connected with their ethics. They believed they could show that the whole world (i.e. the universe) was the planned and providential work of God, that human reason if correct must think in the same way as the divine reason, and that man should therefore accept willingly all that happens.

It must be confessed that the basic principle that everything is providentially planned appears to be asserted rather than argued. It is not known how Zeno tried to establish the omnipotence of God, if he tried at all. But we have an argument of his to support the existence of gods: 'it would be reasonable to honour the gods; it would not be reasonable to honour the non-existent; therefore gods exist'. Cleanthes put forward an argument more interesting than this obvious fallacy:[1]

If one nature is better than another, there must be a nature that is best. If one soul is better than another, there must be a soul that is best. And if one living thing is better than another, there must be a living thing that is best. In such cases there is no run to infinity. So there is no infinite

[1]But in his dialogue *Eudemus* (frag. 33 Rose) Aristotle had argued that libations are made to the dead and oaths sworn by them, that no one makes libations to the absolutely non-existent or swears by them, and that this proves the immortality of the soul. He may have known that his second premise fell short of being established; did Zeno see that his first premise was a *petitio principii*?

progression of living things, any more than there is of natures or souls. But clearly one living thing is better [the Greek word also means 'stronger'], than another, as a horse is better than a tortoise and a bull than a donkey and a lion than a bull. Of all living beings on earth man is the superior and the best in condition of body and mind, and so he would seem to be the supreme and best living being. Yet he can hardly be that, when one sees right away that he walks in wickedness all his days, or if not, for the greater part (if he ever were to acquire virtue, it comes late at life's sunset), and he is subject to disaster and lacks strength and needs a thousand kinds of aid, such as food and shelter and all other care of his body, which stands over him like a cruel tyrant demanding a daily toll and threatening disease and death if there should be no provision for its washing and oiling and clothing and feeding. So man is not a perfect living being, but imperfect and far removed from perfection. What is perfect and best would be superior to man, replete with all the virtues and untouched by any ill. This will be identical with God. Therefore there is a God. (Sextus, *Against the Dogmatists,* 9.88–91.)

This also is fallacious, depending on the ambiguity of the word 'best', used sometimes to mean 'the best that there is', sometimes 'the best that could be'.

Besides this attempted logical proof Cleanthes enumerated reasons which as a matter of fact caused men to believe in gods: the experience of foretelling the future, the greatness of the benefits offered man by the world in which he lives, the terror that arises from storms, lightning, pestilence, earthquakes, etc., the regularity of the movements of the heavenly bodies. All but the third of these reasons had been given by Aristotle in his published dialogue *On Philosophy* (frag. 12 Rose), and it does not appear in any later Stoic author, being no doubt inconvenient for believers in Providence.

Chrysippus modified Cleanthes' logical argument to run as follows:

If there are no gods there can be nothing better than man, as the sole possessor of reason. But it would be foolish arrogance to think there was nothing better in the world than yourself. Then there is something better, and God therefore exists.

He also argued that the maker of the heavenly bodies must be superior to man, who could not make them, and therefore be a God.

In his interesting book *Physics of the Stoics* (1959) S. Sambursky tried to show that in some sense they anticipated many modern ideas. There is a danger of exaggerating the similarity, but it is useful to recognise that they took some steps in the right direction, even although the road they followed was no throughway. To the modern reader much of Stoic physics must seem childishly inadequate or misconceived; the detail is only to be understood if it is seen as dependent on certain primitive conceptions. But for all this he should bear in mind that in some ways Stoic views approached modern ones more nearly than did those of other ancient thinkers. First, they saw the world as a continuum. For us there is a continuum of forces: gravitation binds together the whole of the solar system, while its rotation generates forces that prevent its collapse; for the Stoics the continuum was material, a 'breath' passing through all things and not merely maintaining them, but also giving them their characteristics. Secondly, as we think of overlapping fields of force or superimposed wave motions, they conceived of the 'breath' as having simultaneous states added one to another. Thirdly, they emphasised the change and movement that characterise nature; stability is a secondary phenomenon due to an equilibrium of forces; the world is to be seen as a process leading from birth to consummation.

ULTIMATE PRINCIPLES

Zeno accepted the common view that there were four elemental substances, earth, water, air and fire, and also the common belief that these were mutable: earth could become water, water air, air fire, and vice versa. This appears to be evident: springs bubble up from the earth, water left in a pan disappears into the air, and so does a flame, which will on the other hand not burn if deprived of air. This way of interpreting the world does not require the so-called 'elements' each to have a single form; there were, for example, different kinds of thing that the Greeks called 'air': mist is a visible kind, wind an invisible, just as the air we breathe out is invisible on a warm day, visible on a frosty one. But all forms of 'air' are much more like one another than they are like any kind of 'water'. Similarly the Stoics distinguished various kinds of 'fire'. There was the fire to be seen within a burning object, the flame which is outside it, and the radiance or light that proceeds from the flame. But fire was not all visible: for example, the warmth of a living creature was due to there being fire within it, but one that could not be seen.

The mutability of the elements requires that they cannot be the ultimate principles; there must be something that underlies them. Zeno held that these ultimate principles were two, God and matter. God is active, matter passive; matter has no qualities (although it must be supposed to have extension and also 'resistance to pressure', to distinguish it from mere extension or space), God is *logos,* a word for which there is no English equivalent. *Logos* has many implications, which make it a dangerous tool for philosophers. The noun cognate with the verb *legein* 'to say', not only is it *language,* 'speech', 'expression', it is the *explanation* of a thing, which may be the account or *formula* of its constitution, and the statement of its *purpose.* But to give the grounds for anything is a *rational* activity, and the epithet 'rational' may be supposed to mean what is marked by the use, not merely of reason, but by that of correct reason. Perhaps 'plan' has something of the same ambiguity. A plan may be nothing more than a map which indicates the shape of natural features. In this sense it is theoretically possible to make a plan of Greece. But the plan of a house not only indicates its shape, but implies the intentions of a rational being, its architect. And a plan of campaign does not relate to something static like a house, but to a process of which the later stages are foreseen from the first. So the *logos* that is God by giving shape to matter makes the world and all the things that are in it; it is rational, that is to say the world is not an arbitrary or haphazard construction; and finally the world must be seen as a dynamic process, tending to some kind of consummation, not as a static organisation with a permanent form. This last feature is not a necessary implication of the word *logos,* but it is one that is fundamental to the Stoic way of looking at the universe, and distinguishes them from Platonists and Peripatetics.

God and matter are always conjoined, and their conjunction makes the four elements. It is the *logos* which makes the matter take the form now of fire, now of water and now of earth.

There are many passages in which the Stoic god is said to be a breath (*pneuma*) that passes through all things and fashions them; a breath is elsewhere defined as a mixture of air and fire. The god that makes the world is also sometimes called 'fire that is an artificer (*pyr technikon*)'. Since air and fire can in theory be analysed into combinations of matter and God, the Stoics, seem to be caught in an eternal regress, if God is, as breath or fire, himself a combination of matter and God. The difficulty is so obvious that a misunderstanding may be suspected. The mistake lies in supposing that the word 'God' always denotes the same thing. The falsity of this assumption is apparent since Stoics could call the whole world 'God' (e.g. Chrysippus in Cicero, *Nature of the Gods* 1.39), no less than the immanent force that gave it all its character. Most immediately this force consisted of the 'breath', a combination of air and fire, that penetrated and organised the inert elements of earth and water. But since this material 'breath' that may be called God is a body, it is therefore logically analysed into matter and God. Here is reached the basic meaning of God, not a body, but that which by its association with matter gives rise to the first body and is responsible for its qualities. There is then no regress, if the distinction is preserved between God as a basic principle and God as a body with characteristics given by that basic principle. But it may be doubted whether Stoic authors, when they spoke of God passing through the universe, were always clear in which sense they were using the word, nor would it matter to them, since in either sense the statement was true.

There is one consideration that tells against this solution. God acts upon prime matter, he is the cause (Seneca, *Letters* 65.2) that gives it form; and all causes, according to the orthodox view, are bodies, and act upon bodies. Moreover only bodies can be said to 'be', although incorporeal things have some other sort of quasi-existence. Diogenes Laertes 7,134 says that the ultimate principles are bodies,[1] and there are several passages in handbook summaries or in the writings of opponents where matter is said to be body. Perhaps the solution is this. Any actual body is a compound of matter and *logos*; these principles cannot each *be* body in that sense, yet taken together they are body. This may have been misunderstood to mean that each severally was a body.

Some modern authors identify 'fire the artificer' with God the *logos*. This is not justified. Fire the artificer is a form of the element fire, distinguished by its constructive effects from destructive fire, but just as much a combination of matter and *logos*. It is not a basic principle, but a material thing, perceptible by the senses. The sun was described as 'an intelligent star, fiery with artificer fire', and Cleanthes said that its fire was like the fire to be found in living things; this fire is, of course, that which gives them warmth. All fire needs nourishment; the fire of an animal is fed by converting an exhalation from the blood, the fire of the sun is ignited from the exhalation (evaporation) from the sea.

The use of the word *hylê* (matter) for one of the basic principles recalls the Aristotelian analysis of things into matter and form. But the active, divine *logos* is much more reminiscent of the Platonists with whom Zeno studied. Under the mask of Timaeus in the dialogue of that name, Plato had himself suggested that a divine craftsman made reflections of the Forms appear in a 'Receptacle itself devoid of qualities': thus was constituted the physical world. He did not give the name 'matter' to that receptacle, which was indeed more like space, but later Platonists did. Whether that had happened by Zeno's time cannot be said; it must be confessed that there is no evidence of it.[2] Xenocrates took as his first principles the One, which he also called Zeus and Mind, and the Ever-Changing or the Undeter-

---

[1]So in our mss. but the *Suda* quoting the passage substitutes the word 'incorporeal' for 'bodies'. Aristocles, however, thought Zeno to have believed that both matter and God were bodies (see Eusebius XV p. 816d).

[2]But Aristotle already identified the Receptacle with matter: 'Plato says in *Timaeus* that matter and space are one and the same' (*Physics* 4. 209 b 11).

mined, which later Greeks identified with matter. Zeno's scheme
has a clear similarity with these Academic views, and this was
seen in the second century AD by Aristocles who wrote: 'they say
that the elementary stuff of things is fire, as Heraclitus did, and
that its principles are matter and god, like Plato'.

TOTAL BLENDING

An essential element of Stoic physics was the doctrine of 'total
blending' (*krâsis dï'holôn*). According to this, two substances
might occupy the same space, although each is continuous and
contains no void. These substances retained their identities and
their qualities, so that 'blending' was distinguished from 'fusion',
in which the original qualities are lost. The size of the body so
formed was not determined by adding the sizes of the constitu-
ents; it might be larger or smaller than either. Each constituent
was conceived of as indefinitely elastic: so Chrysippus declared
that a drop of wine could blend with the whole ocean, or even
spread through the whole universe. The importance of the
doctrine lies in the explanation of qualities. These were given
to objects composed mainly of the inert elements, earth and
water, by 'breaths' of the active air and fire, which moved within the space occupied by the object. The complete interpene-
tration of the earth and water by the air and fire gave rise to an
object of which every part was characterised by its own qualities. In the case of a living being, this 'breath' was that particular combination of air and fire that was called *psyche* (life–soul),
and by penetrating all the tissues it made them live tissues.
Similarly in the macrocosm God was conceived as a breath penetrating and controlling and unifying the whole of the world.
This unifying breath was the world's *psyche:* the world was a
living being, as indeed it had been for Plato in the *Timaeus,*
and it was animated by a perfect intelligence. This conclusion is
best seen as an act of faith, inspiring and comforting. The attempts made to confirm it by reasoning seem obvious sophistries,
for example: the intelligent is better than the unintelligent and
the animate than the inanimate; nothing is better than the
world; therefore the world is intelligent and animate. Or again:
nothing without life and reason can generate a living being that
possesses reason; the world generates living and reasoning
beings; therefore the world is living and possesses reason (Zeno

in Cicero, *Nature of the Gods* 2.22). It is not plain what is the relation between the universal breath and the breaths that give individual things their qualities. Perhaps they are best seen as parts of the whole, so that the mixed air and fire of which they are composed will pass in and out of the object as well as move back and forth within it.

The concept of 'total blending' is strange to us, who are accustomed to think of matter not as continuous but as atomic[1] It was found equally strange by other ancient philosophers, who could not stomach the idea that two bodies might occupy the same place. Nevertheless the Stoics maintained that it was one commonly held. After all this is what appears to happen when iron is made red-hot or water mixed with wine. Every part of the iron seems to be fiery, every part of the wine to be watery: we do not see particles of wine and water, or of iron and fire, juxtaposed; on the contrary there seems to be a total blending. That the wine and the water retain their identities was supposed to be established by an experiment: it was claimed that if an oiled sponge is placed in a mixture of wine and water, water is separated out and taken up by the sponge.

TENSION

Closely attached to the idea of the interpenetrating breath is that of 'tension'. The word is first met in the fragments of Cleanthes, where it recurs several times. This may be accidental, but perhaps he introduced it. Tautness may be illustrated by a human muscle or the string of a lyre. The tense muscle keeps its shape even under external pressure, the string not only returns, when plucked, to its original position, but to its tension also owes both its straightness and its sonority. Probably enlarging on such observations the Stoics believed that tension was the cause of all lasting states of things, and indeed of the durability of the things themselves. Tension is what holds things together, from the whole world down to the smallest object in it.

To recognise that there are cohesive forces in nature was important, to suppose them all to be the same force an over-

[1]Consistent with the view of matter as a continuum was the denial of any void within the world. Void was necessary outside the world to allow for its future expansion (see p. 78 below).

simplification. To give them a name was easy, to provide an explanation more difficult. Cleanthes said that tension was 'a stroke of fire'; what he meant by this must be uncertain (Plutarch *Moralia* 1034 D). But the later orthodox view, probably due to Chrysippus, held tension to be primarily a quality of air or of *pneuma* (the 'breath' that is a mixture of air and fire), communicated by them to the objects formed by their interpenetrating mixture with earth and water. This quality was itself explained as the resultant of two equal but opposed motions. The *pneuma* which is mixed with the two inert elements in any physical thing is at once moving outwards towards the surface and inwards towards the centre. The outward movement gives the object size, shape, and other qualities, the inward integrates it, causes it to be one thing, a single substance. These two opposed motions, whose sum results in stability, might be understood in three ways. First, part of the air might move outwards while an equal part moved inwards. The stability would then be like that of Heraclitus' world, where water changes into fire and an equal measure of fire changes into water. Secondly, the whole of the air might move outwards at one instant and inwards at the next, giving what we should call a vibration. Thirdly, there may be no change of place at all, but the 'movements' are what we should call 'forces' acting upon the air. The doctor Galen, discussing muscular tension, uses material provided by the supporters of 'tensional movements'. A body, he says, may be moved in opposite directions by two forces, and remain in the same place: for example a stationary swimmer may be moved downstream by a current, and upstream by his own exertions. Similarly a hovering bird is moved downwards by its weight, upward by the beat of its wings. He then asks, but leaves the question open, whether there is in such cases an alternation of real movement so rapid as to escape the eye or a truly stationary position (*On Muscular Movement* 1.8.).

Which was the Stoic way of thinking? Sambursky supposes they gave the 'vibrating' explanation, but this may be no more than Galen's own suggestion. Philo, who adopts much Stoic doctrine, describes the *pneuma* as proceeding to the surface, turning round, and returning to the starting point (*God's Immutability* 35). He must intend a continuous stream of which at any moment part is moving outward, part turning, part coming back. If this is correct, the swimmer and the bird will represent a thing's inert elements, held in place by the equivalent inward and outward movements of the breath that passes through them.

Since the p*syche* is a physical body it will have its own tension. Just as muscle may be firm, or if its tension is inadequate, slack, so the *psyche* may be firm or slack. A slack muscle is inefficient and a slack *psyche* will be unable to maintain a correct opinion. It is no doubt because a wise man's *psyche* or soul is taut that it alone, according to Chrysippus, survives until the general conflagration: weaker souls collapse and break up.

THE 'CONFLAGRATION'

The belief that the world-process culminated in the conversion of everything to fire, which would die down to become first air, then water,[1] except for a remnant, a seed that would reorganise a new world, identical in every detail and every incident with that of the preceding cycle, a sequence eternally repeated, is a picturesque but strange feature of orthodox Stoicism. The heavenly fires of sun and stars needed their fuel, which was provided by the evaporation of water from the earth and its seas, and it was argued that the water would finally be exhausted and the fire then consume air and earth. Since fire is more tenuous than the other elements the universe must expand in this conflagration; hence there must be empty space outside the world sphere organised as we know it, although there is none within it. Cleanthes thought that in the final stage the world would be all flame, not realising that there cannot be a flame without something to feed it. Chrysippus went further and believed that it would be all light, the most tenuous sort of fire; possibly, since light is associated with knowledge, he thought this the ideal form to be taken by the rational thinking soul of the world when it was rid of its body.

[1] It may cause surprise that the process does not lead to the element most distant from fire, namely earth. The reason may be that as soon as water has appeared the remnant of fire has an inert element on which to work; it converts some water into air, while other parts of the water become earth: thus there arise all four elements required for a world.

THE SYSTEM: NATURAL SCIENCE

Some Stoics claimed that a conflagration had been part of Heraclitus' cosmology, but it seems more likely that they found it possible so to interpret him in order to support their own view than that they derived it from him. One can only guess at their reasons for holding it. Perhaps Zeno believed that fire would necessarily continue to convert other elements into itself so long as fuel remained. But, however arrived at, the doctrine was acceptable because if the world is seen as a process, it is convenient that the process should tend to some end or perfection; at the conflagration the world is at its most perfect, no longer body and soul as it were, but all converted to the kind of fire that had previously given it its qualities. The idea that there are innumerable world cycles, identical in every detail, had already occurred to some Pythagoreans, and Zeno may have known of this: he wrote a book called *Pythagorica*. But whether he borrowed or invented it, it was necessary that if there were successive world-cycles, they should be identical, since Providence, which is responsible for everything, must order the world in the best way possible, and it is plausible that there cannot be two ways equally good.

The arguments in favour of this scheme were not cogent and it involved difficulties: a number of Stoics in the century after Chrysippus doubted or abandoned it (Zeno of Tarsus, Diogenes of Babylon, Boethus of Sidon (see p. 120), Panaetius). But it remained orthodox and was accepted by Seneca and Marcus Aurelius. The former believed in alternate destructions of the world by fire and water (*Questions about Nature*, 3.27); the flood, however, was only a partial liquefaction, drowning 'most of the earth'; it was a catastrophe, the fire was a consummation. The two events, although the poles of the cycle, are not on the same plane.

FATE AND PROVIDENCE

Since the world and its events are entirely determined by God, thought of as a plan, he can be identified with Nature, with Fate, and with Providence. Nature (*physis*) is a dynamic term, 'the way things grow', and Zeno defined Nature as 'a fire that is an artificer, proceeding methodically to generation'. This is the fire that is God, who methodically executes the plan according to which the world and all that is in it change and grow. Fate is a name for the certainty of the process : the plan is inexorably executed. Providence is God's rationality: the process is purposeful. There was no attempt to suggest that God's purposes might be essentially unfathomable to man. God and man have the same sort of reason, although man's reason may fail; God's purposes will be of a sort that a man, if fully intelligent, would approve. His Providence is seen, therefore, as providing for the maintenance and good order of the world, and for its usefulness to man. An implication was that animals had been created for man's benefit. Perhaps the majority of men treat them in a way which assumes this principle, but the Stoics alone in classical antiquity explicitly recognised it. Chrysippus said that the pig had been given a *psyche* (life) to keep its flesh sweet, and had been made fertile to provide man with his meals. The peacock had its tail because both Nature and man were lovers of beauty. This subordination of animals meant that they had no rights against man, who were free to exploit them.

The belief that all events were pre-determined was used to support the truth of prophecy, and even the arts of the astrologer were accepted when they reached the Greek world in the second century BC. It was easy to suppose that in an integrated universe the position of the stars at a man's birth could be consistent with one set only of future events.[1] In general it was argued that it was convenient for man to know his future and that since God was Providence, he must have provided the means by which it could be known. Critics replied that if man could not affect the future it could not profit him to know it; he would get nothing but unnecessary distress through being forced to know in advance of coming misfortunes. This is a superficial objection. The Stoic aims at avoiding emotional reactions to what the world calls 'evil'; it is the unexpected blow or the sudden disappointment that puts one off balance; to be forewarned is to be forearmed.

Just as the rule of Fate made prophecy possible, the success

[1]But some Stoics kept their heads. Diogenes of Babylon admitted that the stars might indicate character, but nothing more. He pointed out that twins often had differing careers. Panaetius had absolutely no use for astrology.

of prophecy was held to argue for the rule of Fate: Chrysippus therefore gave much attention to collecting instances of veridical predictions by methods ranging from oracles to dreams. Clearly even if all predictions could be shown to be true, it would not follow that all events were fated; yet the more events are correctly predicted, the more plausible it becomes that all are pre-determined.

Posidonius wrote five volumes on prophecy and worked out a theoretical basis for it. (Cicero, *On Divination* 1.64, 125ff; 2.35.) In the first place God may be said to cause omens: for example, we know by experience that a formation X in the entrails of a sacrificial victim portends Y; God either causes man to choose a victim that has this formation, or creates the formation in the victim that has been chosen. But this causation is not isolated; it is part of the whole chain of causes that determines all the world's events. Prophecy is not a kind of magic; both the appearance of the portent and the thing portended have natural causes. God understands all of these, men can know only a part, or perhaps only that Y follows X, not why it follows. On this basis professional prophecy rests. Then men often foresee the future in dreams or trances, or at the point of death: this is because the mind 'sees' most clearly when least involved with the body. Another reason is that God communicates with men in their sleep; this argument recognises a common form of dream in the ancient world, in which a God appears with information or advice. Similarly dead persons also appeared as mentors in dreams and it is probably to this that a third phrase refers: 'the air is full of immortal souls, in whom there appear impressed as it were, marks of truth'.

The idea of a 'chain of causes' is not as easy as might appear at first sight. We are inclined to interpret the phrase to mean that an event X determines another event Y, which in turn determines event Z, and so on. This is not what the Stoics meant. Whereas Aristotle often talked as if one could identify the causes of a *thing*, e.g. a house, they insisted that while the cause was a body and the thing it affected a body, that of which it was the cause was an *event*. A knife and flesh are both bodies, a knife is the cause of a cutting of the flesh, an event. Hence the Stoics cannot understand the 'chain of causes' as meaning that X causes Y, which causes Z, and so on. They identified it with

Fate (appealing, according to ancient methods of etymology, to the likeness of the words *heirmos* 'chain' and *heimarmenê* 'Fate'), and so with the will of God. This must be seen as the world-controlling 'breath' in its successive states. These do not cause one another, but the events in the world. Yet although the links in a chain do not cause one another, in some sense they imply one another, for they must fit together. So the chain of causes must 'hang together' in such a way that it could not be otherwise than it is; to change any part or it would be to ruin the whole.

The 'soul'

The Greek word *psyche* is conventionally and misleadingly translated by 'soul'. It is rather *life*, or the cause of life, and in a human being sensation and perception, emotion and thought are all part of life if it is fully present; they are therefore all activities of the *psyche*. Since life is a characteristic of the living animal, its death is supposed by some to mean that the cause of life no longer exists: on the other hand there are those who feel it illogical that the cause of life should itself suffer death, and believe that it persists when the body dies; and since we do not normally wish our own death or that of our friends, there is an emotional reason for believing that the *psyche,* whose activities we value, should survive and continue to exercise them. Such a belief is usually implied by the word *soul;* it is not implied by *psyche,* although in fact many Greeks did believe in its survival, and indeed in its immortality. Survival of the *psyche* is more difficult for those who, like the Stoics, think it material.[1] When it leaves the body it must be found some local habitation, where it will be subject to physical dangers. Moreover, the Stoics had little reason for wanting the *psyche* to survive. Death was not for them an evil, which an after-life might diminish; the world

[1]Zeno had been unable to conceive of an immaterial *psyche,* as Plato had done, partly because he refused to believe that anything incorporeal was full being, but also because he could not see how anything incorporeal could affect the material body or be affected by it. Popular thought had always conceived of the *psyche* in physical terms, as a tenuous kind of matter, and Epicurus thought in the same way. The Stoics were therefore doing nothing strange in believing in a *psyche* that was material and liable to destruction.

too in which men live was entirely governed by Providence, so no after-life was needed as a recompense. They had then no real interest in survival, although it was orthodox to suppose a limited one.[1] The *psyche*, which was a mixture of air and fire 'in tension', would hold itself together for a time, contracted into a spherical shape and risen to the upper air: the weaker souls would break up first and only those of the ideal wise men would persist until finally caught up in the conflagration that would end the world-cycle. We are given no picture of the life of these disembodied souls, such as is found in the Platonic myths, for there was indeed little that a Stoic could say about it.

For the living man the *psyche* is a 'breath', a compound of air and 'constructive' fire, that extends throughout his body, with which it is totally blended, giving life and warmth, growth and maintenance. But there is a part, called the *hêgemonikon* or centre of command, lodging in the heart,[2] which is the seat of sensation, assent, impulse, passion, thought and reason. From this there extend seven breaths to the eyes, ears, mouth, nose and skin to convey the incoming stimuli which cause sensation, to the organs of speech to set them in motion, and to the sex-organs for the reason, it may be guessed, that they are the channel by which life is transmitted. It would seem consistent that other breaths should be the cause of other movements, and this was Cleanthes' view; but for some reason Chrysippus disagreed, saying that walking was due to an extension of the *hêgemonikon*

[1]Panaetius probably did not believe in any survival, and Marcus Aurelius tended to think that the *psyche* would break up like the body.

[2]Plato had placed thought in the brain, but Zeno follows an older tradition. In Homer thought and emotion were in the lungs, for Empedocles thought was the blood round the heart. Even Aristotle made the heart the centre from which the *psyche* acts. Chrysippus pointed to the effect of emotion on the heart. Besides some frivolous arguments he observed after Zeno that speech (*logos*) came from the chest, and that reason (*logos*) would also be found there. This argument would suggest that the lungs rather than the heart were the seat of the *hêgemonikon*, but he had an easy way with anatomy. He was aware that the doctors had shown that nerves ran from the brain, but his belief in the primacy of the heart was not shaken: the brain, he said, was only an intermediary source of movement. (Galen, *On the Views of Hippocrates and Plato*. 2.5.)

itself to the feet. Perhaps he felt that a movement originated by the *hêgemonikon* did not require a separate part of the *psyche* to explain it, whereas the external stimuli of sensation needed permanent independent parts to convey them to the centre of command. But if he thought like that there seems no reason for maintaining a separate part of *psyche* to account for speech.[1]

To explain in material terms the *psyche* and its functions was an impossible undertaking, but one which had to be attempted. Zeno argued that the *psyche* must be the factor on whose withdrawal from the body an animal died; an animal died when the breath, with which it was born, was withdrawn; and so the *psyche* must be this breath. That breath was more than air was evidenced by its warmth, which showed that some fire too was contained in it. In the living animal this breath was 'nourished' by exhalations from the blood, a doctrine for which Cleanthes found precedent in Heraclitus. One or the other compared the *psyche's* permanence in change with that of a river, always the same river although its waters flow past and are ever new. Critics objected that this picture made it difficult to understand memory, for an impression made on moving water must pass away. And it is on memory, of course, that all the operations of reason are built.

A question on which there is no information is how this breath which is the *psyche* is related to what an animal breathes in and out through its nostrils. But there is evidence about its first beginnings. Chrysippus held that while in the womb the child's existence was like that of a plant—probably he thought that neither had any sensations—and it was therefore not under the control of *psyche* but of 'nature' (*physis*).[2] On birth the shock of the cold outer air converted this *physis* to *psyche* (*psychein* means to chill), just as glowing steel is tempered by immersion in water. Both *physis* and *psyche* are breaths, but *psyche* is more tenuous and warmer, strange characteristics to be caused by cold.

[1] Panaetius saw this (p. 128).

[2] The word *physis* may seem to be a chamaeleon. It is the way a thing grows and is organised. The *physis* of a man is quite different from that of a plant. But in some contexts the word may be restricted to mean the 'nature' of a plant; etymology is here involved, for a plant is a *phyton*.

Sensation was supposed to occur through a contact in the sense-organ between the object sensed and the 'breath' which extended from the central command-centre. The only complications arose over the senses of sight and hearing, which perceive things at a distance. Sound was correctly explained as a spherical wave in the air set in motion by the origin of the noise and impinging on the ear. Sight was more difficult. Chrysippus supposed that contact between the outer air and the breath that extended to the pupil of the eye set up a state of tension in a conical field of air at the base of which lay the object seen. The pressure exerted by the object on this base resulted in a corresponding pressure at the cone's apex, just as pressure is transmitted along a stick, and so a kind of print of the object was transferred to the tentacle of the command centre. But this was not all: the air must be illuminated, if vision was to occur: the light mixed with it will share its tension. A further complication was that the eye was itself supposed to emit fiery rays: their function when it is light is not clear, unless they increased the air's tension; but when it is dark, they enabled the eye to see the darkness. They may help to explain why some people see better than others.

PERCEPTION AND KNOWLEDGE[1]

If a philosopher is to establish any firm conclusions, if an ordinary man is to have any assurance of how to act, they must both start from something they know to be true. Zeno found this in what he called *phantasia kataléptiké*, or 'cognitive presentation'. The question whether such a thing existed was for a couple of centuries to be the subject of animated debate between the Stoics, who maintained it, and the sceptical Academy, who denied it. We must start by considering what was intended by the phrase.

A *phantasia* is what happens in a percipient when something 'becomes apparent'; it was described by Zeno as the 'making of

[1]Many modern authors treat the Stoic theory of perception and knowledge as part of logic. The Stoics themselves took it to be psychology and so part of 'physics'. Cicero, *Academica Posteriora* 1.40, includes the theory under logic, but this is in a critical account derived from Antiochus, who divided philosophy on an Academic–Peripatetic basis.

a print' in the *psyche;* Cleanthes took this literally, as if the imprint were like that of a seal on wax, but Chrysippus interpreted the word to mean an 'alteration' of the *psyche,* or rather of the command-centre in the *psyche.* Whereas one imprint will obliterate another, these vague 'alterations' can persist alongside one another; one could see an analogy in the way a thing may become first hotter, then more solid, without losing the heat first acquired. We should be inclined to regard this 'appearance' as a mental event, associated of course with physical changes in the brain. For the Stoics the *psyche* is material, and so changes in it are physical; a mental event is a physical event. Let us then consider what happens if something in the external world 'becomes apparent'. Aëtius gives this as Chrysippus' view:

> A presentation (*phantasia*) is a happening that occurs in the *psyche*, displaying both itself and what causes it. For example when by vision we look on what is white, what has occurred in the *psyche* through the act of seeing is an affect, and because of this affect we can say that there is a white object which affects us . . . the presentation displays itself and also what has caused it (4.12, 1).

In other words the *psyche* of the percipient is aware of the change it has undergone, but it also perceives the external object: and this perception is part of the change.

The preceding account presumes that there is an external object causing the presentation and revealed by it. This was not always maintained; the word *phantasia* was sometimes applied to dreams and hallucinations. The account would also need some modification if the presentation were one which arose not through the senses but through mental activity: for example, it may become apparent that the sun is larger than the earth. This is a presentation about the external objects sun and earth but, although it reveals something about them, it is not directly caused by them.

Further, if we perceive an external object we may perceive it correctly or incorrectly; and whereas mental activity may lead to the perception that the sun is larger than the earth, it has also led men to the false perception that the earth is larger than the sun. In other words a presentation may be true or false. There is needed some mark by which the true may be distinguished from the false; what that mark was will appear from the elucidation of a simile used by Zeno.

> But you deny that anyone except a wise man knows anything. And indeed Zeno used to show this by gesture. Holding up his hand, open and with fingers outstretched, he would say 'a presentation is like that'. Then he contracted his fingers a little: 'assent is like that'. Then he closed his hand completely, making a fist of it, and said that that was apprehension: it was from this comparison that he gave the name *katalêpsis* (grasping, apprehension, cognition), not used before, to the thing in question. But when he had brought up his left hand and grasped his fist with it tight and hard, he would say that knowledge was a thing of that sort, and possessed by none but the wise (Cicero, *Academica Priora* 2.144).

It appears from this that knowledge is distinguished from mere cognition by being permanent, unshakeable, locked in as it were. But the man who apprehends a thing does grasp the truth, for the moment at least, although his grasp may falter. He is right and is confident that he is right, but that belief may be shaken by considerations that he has not taken into account.

Turning now to the beginning of the image, we see that presentation is represented as purely receptive. As Sextus Empiricus puts it, it does not lie with the subject, but with the object that causes the presentation, that he is affected as he is. The percipient must be ready to receive; for example, he must open his eyes if he is to see—this corresponded to holding out a hand—but what he perceives depends on what is there to be perceived. This analysis is not applicable to presentations that do not come through the senses but stem from the mind. A presentation that the sun is eclipsed by the interposition of the moon must be created by the inventor of that doctrine; or a presentation that it is desirable to start a conspiracy to make oneself king must be created by the would-be conspirator. It must be confessed that much that was said by Stoics about presentations is properly applicable to sense-presentations only. But this is partially excusable, since they held that these were basic. The mind was at birth like a blank sheet of paper; it had potentialities but no content. The first presentations it received came through the senses, and unless some of these could be accepted as reliable, what was later built on them must be unreliable too.

After presentation there comes assent. The partial closing of the fingers represents a voluntary act on the part of the subject; and what he assents to is the presentation. Here there is a difficulty, already raised by Arcesilaus (see p. 91). A presentation is a physical change in the *psyche;* how can one assent to such a thing? Assent should be to a proposition; it is that which is true or false. This is a valid criticism of Stoic language, but perhaps not destructive of the meaning. A presentation reveals itself: that is to say a man is aware of a change in his *psyche,* and there is no question of his giving or withholding his assent to that awareness. But the presentation also reveals that which causes it; that is to say, it does not merely appear to him that he is seeing, e.g. an apple; it appears to him that there is an apple which he is seeing. Here there is contained something to which assent is applicable. The man may say 'There appears to be an apple, and I assent: there is an apple', or 'There appears to be an apple, but I do not assent: there is no apple, or there may be no apple'. This proposition 'there is an apple' is not identical with the presentation, but is in some sense included in it, and put before the mind by it. Hence although it may be inaccurate, it is psychologically intelligible to say that one assents to a presentation.

But how is one to know that assent is correct? We must look at the next stage of Zeno's simile. Apprehension or cognition is the grasp of a 'cognitive presentation', and that was defined as 'a presentation stamped and impressed, arising from an existent thing and according with the existent thing and such as would not arise from a non-existent'. An existent thing, moreover, was explained as one that gives rise to a cognitive presentation. In other words, there is a reciprocal relation between 'what exists' and cognition. If we apprehend something, it exists: if something exists, it can be apprehended. It is a mistake to look for any test by which it can be established that a presentation is cognitive. There are of course conditions that make this more likely or less likely: sobriety and a good light are more favourable to correct assent than drunkenness and shadow. But in the last resort the cognitive presentation is recognised by some peculiar quality indicated by the use of such words as 'evident', and 'striking'. There are some presentations which are self-evidently true. That is what an ordinary man believes: it is unusual that he should doubt the truth of a presentation; normally he has no reservations whatever about saying that the sun is shining or that he is travelling in a boat or that a bull is approaching him. He is certain that these presentations arise from real, existing things and correspond to them. These cognitive presentations are, then, the test of truth because they provide an answer to the question: How do you know? For example, how do you know that the sun is shining? I know because I have a cognitive presentation that it is shining.

The account so far has passed over certain problems that deserve a brief mention.[1] 1. *Katalêptikê*, the word translated 'cognitive', means more literally either 'capable of grasping' or 'capable of being grasped'. The evidence shows that grasping is something done by the percipient; but it is not clear what he grasps: the presentation or the external object. My own belief is that he does both, primarily grasping the presentation but more importantly apprehending thereby the object that caused it. 2. If one has a cognitive presentation, does one necessarily assent to it? Some 'young Stoics' thought that one did not, but there is no evidence what the view of Zeno or Chrysippus was. 3. Cicero says that Zeno found the criterion of truth in cognition. Some scholars have seen here a significant difference from Chrysippus' view that found it in the cognitive presentation. I do not believe this to be right.

From the presentations that arise through sense-impressions there automatically follow certain other changes in the *psyche*. First memory, which is the storing away of the presentation; next experience, the accumulation of similar memories; this leads to the formation of what were called *prolêpseis*, 'preconceptions' or 'preliminary conceptions', and from these there comes into being 'reason', or the capacity for reasoning, and this in its turn will give rise to rational presentations. Reason is recognisable in a child of seven and is fully developed by the age of fourteen. It is probably reason that allows man to acquire new conceptions on the basis of those that have come through

[1]See A. A. Long (ed.), Problems in Stoicism, pp. 13–18.

his sensations. Thus from his conception of 'man' he may conceive 'dwarf' and 'giant' and 'man with no hands' by the processes of diminution, magnification, and deprivation. From his experience of separate objects or of successive events he can conceive 'space' and 'time'.

The details of all this development from the primary presentations are not dealt with in our sources, and it may be that the Stoics had little success in working them out. There is a difficult step from 'preconceptions', which must be generalising ideas about things we have seen, e.g. 'man is a thing that is two-footed, two-armed, featherleess, etc., etc.', to the capacity for reasoning; but the same hiatus is found in Aristotle. There is also a puzzle about the formation of moral concepts. Diogenes Laertius reports that according to the Stoics 'there is a natural conceiving of something just and good'. Since the mind is at birth a blank sheet of paper, this conception must be stimulated by sense-experience, although it would not arise unless a man's nature were such that he is equipped to make the inference from his observations. The process imagined must not be unlike that by which the Platonist proceeds from observation of many beautiful things to conceiving the Form of Beauty. Several passages show that, for the Stoic, acquaintance with the primarily natural things that men call 'good' and with actions that men call 'just' causes the mind to reach by analogy the conceptions to which Zeno had attached the words (Cicero, *De Finibus* 3.33, Seneca, *Letters* 120.4, Polybius 6.6).

To recapitulate, the Stoic theory of knowledge posits a process by which various mental operations build a structure upon data provided by the presentations that the senses give. Reliable presentations are recognisable and any man is therefore capable of grasping the truth. But such grasp is not knowledge in the full sense of the word, since he may let it slip, overcome perhaps by other conclusions based on unreliable presentations or faulty operations of the mind. True knowledge is to be seen as an interlocking structure in which all the members are sound and support one another. Although this outline of the Stoic system is clear, the details are, owing to lack of evidence, obscure. In particular one would like to know more of the way in which intellectual presentations were treated. Epictetus speaks of a presentation 'that the mysteries were introduced to improve life' (*Discourses,* 3.21.15): this will in his opinon be true, but will it be immediately recognisable as true, or only through a process of argument? Whatever the answer, the basis of the whole system is to be found in the primary presentations given by the senses. It was therefore against these that the main attack of the Academy was directed.

The Academy was turned to scepticism by Arcesilaus, a younger contemporary of Zeno; but the most influential figure was Carneades who, in the first half of the second century BC, advanced the attractive view that although there was no certainty, there might be probability. At the same time he showed by his treatment of particular problems how difficult it was to attain even probability. But the question fundamentally at issue between the Stoics and the sceptical Academy was whether there were any cognitive presentations; that is whether there was any true presentation of such a nature that an identical one could not arise which was false, either because it misrepresented the thing which caused it or because it represented as real something which was non-existent. The battle was fought on the level of sense-presentations, from which all the illustrations were drawn.

THE MEANING OF 'BEING'

There are some questions which we might regard as belonging to metaphysics, as concerned with the meaning of the verb 'to be'. For Stoics metaphysics was not a distinct part of philosophy, and its subject matter was seen as falling to the realm of physics. It will therefore be justifiable to end this account of Stoic physics with a brief treatment of these questions.

One of the problems that exercised philosophers of the fourth century BC was what sort of things could properly be said to 'be'. On the one side were those who maintained that material entities were the only things that 'are'; on the other Plato urged that no material thing 'really is', because it is always changing at every moment and 'to be' implies stability. But in his late dialogue the *Sophist* (247 E) he suggests that a mark of 'being' was the capacity to act or to be acted upon. This was accepted by the Stoics who, however, also thought that only what was corporeal had this capacity. Plato had used his definition to make the materialist admit that soul (*psyche,* see p. 82) and wisdom

91

and justice 'were'. This caused the Stoics no embarrassment. *Psyche* was for them a corporeal thing, and so in a sense were wisdom and justice. For if it was said that wisdom or justice caused a man to perform such-and-such an action, what was meant thereby was not some abstraction but something in him that might be called his wisdom or his justice. These were states of his *psyche*, physical conditions, and therefore as corporeal as it was itself. Only body, they believed, could act upon body, and what was not body could not be acted upon.

If 'being' is defined in this way, it can be predicated only of material things, although that class will include much that we do not usually think of as material, e.g. qualities of mind and character possessed by individuals. But there are many immaterial objects of thought which it would be absurd to suppose absolutely non-existent. Some other word than 'be' to indicate their manner of existence would have been useful, but none was exclusively decided upon. The most important of these immaterial things are time, space, place and void, and the meaning of words and sentences (see p. 96). None of these can either act upon anything else nor be acted upon. A meaning can of course act if it is embodied by being spoken or written down or believed (for that implies a physical change in the man who believes it), but *per se* it is inert.

Time and void are both continua and the former is the more interesting. Time, said Zeno, is the interval of movement or change. That may be understood as follows. Any change is from a situation at an instant A, to a situation at an instant B; the interval between those instants is time. It is therefore an accompaniment of change, not something with an independent being of its own. Chrysippus modified Zeno's definition by saying that time was the interval of the change of the world. This had the advantage of showing that time, like the world, had neither beginning nor end and of providing a unified single time common to all men. Chrysippus saw also that 'now' had, strictly speaking, no extension but meant the limit between past and future time. Loosely, however, it was used to cover a period, some of which was past and some yet to come, a period without any definite boundaries. This period is what we mean by 'the present time', constituted of some past time and some future time. Different verbs were used to distinguish the modes of existence of present time on the one hand and past and future on the other. Present time was felt to be more real, just because it is present, whereas the others are no longer or not yet present. The same two verbs were used to mark the difference between true and false propositions, e.g. between 'I am sitting' when I am sitting and the same proposition when I have risen to my feet. But the distinction does not solve the problems to which it calls attention. A proposition is the meaning of a set of words and that meaning's existence is independent of its truth-value. The Stoics were probably misled by the common Greek failure to disentangle 'what is' and 'what is true'.

THE 'CATEGORIES'

There are four terms 1. substrate, 2. qualified thing (*poion*), 3. thing in a certain state (*pôs echon*), 4. thing in a certain relative state (*pros ti pôs echon*), which occur from time to time in Stoic literature. The only systematic treatments to survive that associate them are in Plotinus and in later Peripatetic commentators, anxious to show this to have been an absurd doctrine, inferior to that of the ten Aristotelian categories. It is not certain that the Stoics used the word categories of their terms, and there can be no presumption that they served the same purpose as the Aristotelian categories. Plotinus calls them 'classes of what is', but although they all refer to things that 'are', i.e. are corporeal substances, the classification, if it is one, does not seem to be of ways in which they 'are'.

Any object must be a qualified thing, and its qualities are material, being breaths passing through its substance, in other words it is a combination of substrate and qualities. A man's qualities are partly general and make him a man, and partly individual and make him the particular man he is. A similar division can be made with regard to any object; it is qualified generally as a ship, a dove, or a stone, and individually as a particular ship, dove or stone. The Stoics held that no two objects were identical, since the same individual quality could not attach to two substances. Besides the qualities that make him a human being, a man must at any moment be in certain states, sleeping or waking, standing or walking, angry or calm, and so on. Even lifeless objects have such shifting states; a stone may be hot or cold. As these come and go, there must be physical changes in the subject. But there are other states which are relative to external things, and these come and go without necessarily involving a physical change in the subject. For example, a man who is taller than his son is in a relative state, which can be ended without any change in him by the growth of his son. But the relative state of the son, who is shorter than his father, may be altered by a change in himself, as he grows.

The most frequently used of these terms seems to be 'in a certain state'. All functions of the *psyche,* e.g. presentation, assent, memory, knowledge, each different passion or virtue could be described as 'the *psyche* in a certain state', all being understood as various physical conformations of the material *psyche*. A man's actions can similarly all be described by saying that he is 'in a certain state'. All qualities also are due to the presence in an object of a 'breath in a certain state', that state being different for each different quality.

An instance of the use of the distinction between the terms is provided by Chrysippus' treatment of Aristo's position that one and the same virtue was given different names according to the fields in which it was employed (see p. 42). He argued that the various virtues differed by being qualified things, i.e. each had its own permanent quality, not by being in relative states, i.e. given their distinctive names for different external relations not for different internal constitution. It is noteworthy that the virtue, although an individually qualified thing, is also 'breath in a certain state'. The virtue itself is unchanging, but the breath that constitutes it is not always in that state which is virtue. Before a man becomes virtuous that breath must be in some other state.

5

The System: Logic

Diogenes Laertius lists 311 volumes by Chrysippus on logic, more than a third of his total writing. Little will however be said here on Stoic logic, because it had a limited influence in antiquity and surviving information is fragmentary. Nevertheless it clearly was both original and important; moreover the field covered was wider than that suggested by the modern word 'logic'. Logic for the Stoics, being the science of *logos*, which means both speech and reason, was concerned to examine not only the validity of various forms of reasoning and the relation of words to things, but also the structure of language. Even rhetoric was not left wholly unconsidered, being regarded as an expanded form of 'dialectic', or the science of arguing correctly. But this view did not encourage giving it attention: dialectic was the essential subject of study. Cleanthes wrote an Art of Rhetoric, and so did Chrysippus, but according to Cicero, 'if anyone should want to be struck dumb, he should read nothing else'. The first object of the practitioner of oratory, such as Cicero, was to move and persuade his audience; he might argue logically, but that was only one of his tools.

Although both Zeno and Cleanthes wrote something on logic, it was Chrysippus who systematically developed the subject. It is likely enough that we should often be impatient with his attempts, if we had them, to deal with logical puzzles and he seems to have made some mistakes that look elementary today, yet his work contained many anticipations of the logical discoveries of the last century and can still suggest interesting problems.

Aristotle, although he regarded individual things as primary substance, had been concerned mainly with the relations between universal terms, such as are for him the prime concern of science. 'If all A is B, and all B is C, then all A is C', is his fundamental syllogism; in this sentence all three variables (A, B, and C) must be universals: typical instances are 'king', 'man', and 'mortal'; if they are substituted for the variables, we have as a specimen of this kind of syllogism 'if all kings are men and all men are mortal, then all kings are mortal'. For the Stoics the only thing that 'exists' is the individual: the universal is nothing but a mental construct. Accordingly they developed a logic that would treat statements about individual things. It began with a triple distinction between 1, the spoken word, which is material, being a configuration of air, and significant; 2, what it signifies, which is something immaterial, being 'what it says' or 'what it means'; 3, the material reality to which the meaning refers. Sextus gives as an example the word 'Dion' (*Against the Dogmatists*, viii. 12), but the point is clearer if we take a sentence such as 'Dion is running'. It is obvious that the meaning of the words (which will themselves vary according to the language of the speaker), is not to be confused with the material reality of a running Dion. For the words may both be uttered and have their meaning although Dion is sitting down. In this sentence the meaning (*lekton*), or to use the name of this particular kind of meaning, the proposition (*axioma*), is true or false: true if Dion is running when the words are uttered, false if he is not. But the words may have meanings that are not true or false: for example, the meaning of a question, a command, or a wish is neither true nor false. 'Is Dion running?' and 'Run, Dion' both mean something, but not anything that can be confirmed or denied. Yet both phrases also refer to a material event, running by Dion. It is not known whether any Stoics found a difficulty in the fact that the event may not occur, but be no more than something that is imagined.

Another possible difficulty is that men sometimes utter sentences that are generalisations and do not appear to refer to material realities, e.g. 'two and two make four'. A way out is provided by the Stoic treatment of definition. 'Man is a mortal rational animal' can be restated as 'If any X is a man, that X is a mortal rational animal'; thus what appeared to be a proposition about a universal 'man' becomes a proposition about the material individual X (Sextus, *Against the Dogmatists*, xi. 8). Moreover when we say that X is mortal, by 'mortal' we mean that he has a bodily constitution (his own particular constitution) incapable of permanent survival. Similarly '$2+2=4$' can be restated as 'If any X is two things and any Y is two things, then X and Y are four things'.

THE SYSTEM: LOGIC

The Stoic recognition of meaning as an independent element seems sound. Aristotle had supposed that meaning was identical with thought; what words signify is a thought in the mind of the speaker. Specious though this is, it cannot be right, since by a slip of the tongue a man may utter words the meaning of which has never been entertained in his mind. 'Corinth lies east of Athens' has a meaning which may have been completely absent from the mind of the man who utters those words while intending to say 'Corinth lies west of Athens'.

The primacy of the individual appears again in the Stoic treatment of syllogism. Although they did sometimes use the Aristotelian forms of syllogism (e.g. Chrysippus quoted by Plutarch, *Moralia,* 1041 A), since philosophers cannot avoid dealing in generalisations and the use of universal terms, they investigated a different type of inference, which connected not terms but propositions. Propositions need not of course concern individual material realities, but it is significant that those used by the Stoics to give instances of valid inference are of that kind, e.g. 'the sun is shining', 'it is day'. So a typical Stoic syllogism is: 'if the sun is shining, it is day; but the sun is shining; therefore it is day'. The relation is one of the two propositions. Although the Peripatetics were aware of such syllogisms they had little interest in them. Only in the nineteenth century was their importance appreciated by logicians, who had no knowledge of their Stoic forerunners. Chrysippus recognised five basic forms; each linked a pair of propositions, which he represented by the variables 'the first', 'the second'. Using the more convenient modern symbols p and q, they may be set out as follows:

1. If p, q. But p. $\therefore$ q.
2. If p, q. But not q. $\therefore$ Not p.
3. Not both p and q. But p. $\therefore$ Not q.
4. Either p or q. But p. $\therefore$ Not q.
5. Either p or q. But not p. $\therefore$ q.

These forms were called 'undemonstrated', because their validity cannot be proved, except in so far as it cannot be denied without breaking the law of contradiction. That they are valid is immediately apprehended. Chrysippus was aware that forms 1 and 2 can be deduced from form 3 if its first premise takes the shape 'not both p and not q'. The object of his classification therefore was not the theoretical one of establishing a minimum basis for argument, but the practical one of listing schemes of inference that are accepted at sight as being valid. He then went on to pay much attention to establishing other more complicated patterns of inference, the validity of which could be proved by the assumption of one of the undemonstrated forms. Ancient writers who report this thought it unprofitable pedantry and give little information about his procedures.

There are many examples to show that the Stoics made practical use of these syllogisms which, incidentally, have the advantage of accommodating verbs of all kinds, whereas the Aristotelian variety admits only the copula that joins a predicate to a subject. Cicero, for instance, quotes an argument used by Chrysippus and others.

If (a) gods exist and (b) do not foretell the future, either (c) they do not love us, or (d) they do not know what will happen, or (e) they do not think it would profit us to know or (f) they do not think that it would accord with their dignity to tell us, or (g) they are unable to tell us. But it is not true that they do not love us, nor that they do not know what will happen, etc. [A reason is given for rejecting each alternative.] Therefore it is not true that the gods exist and do not foretell the future. But the gods exist. Therefore they foretell the future. (*On Divination* 1.82.)

Here there is a combination of forms 2 and 3, which can be set out schematically as follows:

If $a+b$, either c or d or e or f or g. But not c or d or e or f or g. $\therefore$ Not both a and b. But a. $\therefore$ Not b.

Clearly these forms of syllogism would be of no practical importance without an assurance of the truth of their premises. Some attention was paid to this problem, but again information is scanty. The difficulty lies in the major premise, which is a compound proposition. How is it to be known whether 'If p,q' or 'Either p or q' is true? Sometimes there may

be a logical necessity that establishes the truth of such propositions, but often they are of a sort exemplified by 'If this
woman has milk in her breasts, she has borne a child', or 'If this
man has a wound in his heart, he will die'. If it is asked how
the truth of either of these propositions can be known, the
answer must be that it is known by induction. To take the first
of them, experience records that innumerable women with
milk have previously borne children and that no woman with
milk has not borne a child. The fact that this woman has milk
becomes for the Stoics a sign that this woman has previously
had a child. This is certainly the way in which men think.

Many later writers regarded the Stoic logic as a rival to
Aristotelian and denigrated it with little attempt to understand
it. This was a mistake; it is in the main not an alternative but
a complement, and the propositional syllogism is today recognised as being logically prior to the syllogism of terms. But
although Stoic logic can be properly contrasted with that of
Aristotle, there is little evidence that he exercised any important influence on its development. Nowhere can Chrysippus be
detected arguing against Peripatetic views; rather he seems to
ignore them. On the other hand he often pursues problems
that had exercised the Megarian logicians, including problems
of possibility and necessity, and ancient sources represent him
as endeavouring to correct these predecessors. The meagre
accounts of that school use the Stoic technical terms, which
often differ from those used by Aristotle. This may mean only
that those accounts come through Stoic intermediaries, but
there is at least a chance, if not a probability, that the Stoics
adopted them from the Megarians; in either case it is evidence
of their interest in the work of that school.

Since 'meanings' can be identified only through the words
that indicate them, there was a tendency to confuse the examination of *lekta* with that of speech. This had a happy result
in the development of grammatical analysis.[1] The recognition
and naming of the parts of speech, the cases of nouns, and the
tenses of the verb was largely a Stoic achievement, adopted by
Crates of Mallos (early second century BC) and after him with

[1] On Stoic grammar see R. H. Robins, *Ancient and Medieval
Grammatical Theory* (London, 1951) pp. 25–36.

slight modifications by succeeding grammarians. Unfortunately the Stoics were unable to achieve the difficult feat of separating grammatical analysis, which concerns the forms of words and their possible relations, from the analysis of meaning. Thus they distinguished as separate parts of speech proper names and common nouns, a distinction of meaning not of grammar.

6

Fate and Free Will, Providence and Evil

Belief in an omnipotent Fate, divine and providential, is hard to combine with recognising the existence of evil, whether that means wickedness or what the ordinary man calls bad, for example pain, disease, war and famine. Both critics and defenders of Stoicism tended to confuse the two kinds of evil, and they had the excuse that the second kind is often the result of wickedness. Nevertheless the problems presented by the existence of moral badness in an order created by God are not the same as those which arise from the presence of what is in itself unwelcome, but not morally evil. It is desirable therefore to keep the two kinds apart.

In his Hymn to Zeus, Cleanthes declared that Zeus wills everything except the actions of bad men, but that these are fitted by him into his scheme. It is self-taught folly that causes wicked acts. The bad man appears as an independent originator of some happenings which God, who had no hand in devising them, is clever enough to turn to serve his purposes. Alluring though such a view may be, it is not easy to hold in conjunction with the dogma that God is the immanent determining element in all physical objects, for these must include the wicked man and his mind. Whether Cleanthes tried to defend the position we do not know, but Chrysippus saw the difficulty and tried to meet it. On the one hand, according to him, everything that happens is fated, i.e. predetermined and according to the plan of the universe. In Book I of *On Nature* he wrote:

Since the management of all there is directs things in this way, it is necessary that we should be as we are, whatever that may be, whether we are sick, contrary to our own natural condition, or maimed, or have become scholarly or artistic . . . consistently with this we shall speak in the same way about our virtue and our wickedness and in general about our crafts or lack of them . . . for no detail, not even the smallest, can happen otherwise than in accordance with universal nature and her plan.

Plutarch, who quotes this (*Moralia* 1049 F), adds: 'that universal nature and nature's plan are Fate and Providence and Zeus, is known even in the antipodes'.

On the other hand, the actions of men are 'attributable to them'. At first sight this looks like allowing them free will, inconsistently with the complete determinism of the passage just quoted. But this is not so, if to say that an action done of man's free will means that he could have chosen not to do that action. An 'attributable' action is something different. Chrysippus illustrated his position by comparing what happens when someone gives a push to a cylinder at rest at the top of a slope. It rolls down, but the cause of its rolling is not merely the push: that is an 'antecedent' cause. The determining cause is the roundness of the cylinder, for the same antecedent cause applied to a cube would not set it going; the cube's squareness would be the determining cause of its stability. Similarly with a man: the exterior world gives rise to presentations, but the reaction to any presentation depends on the condition of the man's *pysche*. The presentation is the antecedent cause of his action, but since the determining cause is to be found in his psyche, the action is attributable to him.

But to say that the action is attributable to the man is not to say that he could have acted otherwise. The rolling of the cylinder is attributable to its roundness, but the cylinder cannot do anything but roll. To suppose that the condition of a man's *psyche* similarly determines his reaction to external circumstances is less absurd than might appear without reflection. A teacher of mathematics, for example, who knows that the side and diagonal of a rectangle are incommensurable, will teach that to his pupils, if the occasion arises; he will not try to show them to be commensurable. But once it is admitted that some actions are predetermined by the 'make-up' of the person who performs them, it is difficult to argue that any are not so determined. Inability to predict whether the mathematician will after school watch television, may be due to nothing more than an inadequate knowledge of his *psyche*.

If a man's action is determined, as Chrysippus held, in this way, how did the condition of his *psyche* arise? Aristotle, recognising that an agent often cannot act in any other way than he does, answered that he had earlier had a real choice, but by exercising it repeatedly in the same way had established a pattern from which he could no longer break out. This line was not open to Chrysippus. Although past decisions and past actions must have brought about the present state of the *psyche,* those past decisions were themselves determined by the state of the *psyche* at the relevant times. All these decisions were attributable to the man, and in a sense voluntarily undertaken; but he was never in a position when he could in fact have taken any other decision than the one he did take. It follows that in the last analysis a man's character is formed not by any choice between open alternatives, but by his environment and the impressions made on him by the external world. These are all due to Fate, which therefore determines what he is. When it is said that an action is attributable to its doer, that means that it is his action, it could not occur without his decision, or in the Stoic terminology without his assent to a presentation and the consequent impulse to act. These things are the determining cause, but they are themselves determined.

It has been maintained that Chrysippus was attempting to combine two things that are logically inconsistent, a belief in rigorous determinism and the truth of 'the psychological experience of freedom in thought and action'. In the Chrysippean fragments we have, there is no talk of this experience, although Zeno's contemporary Epicurus had been very much aware of it. Chrysippus seems rather to have been concerned to maintain the principle that man must accept the responsibility for his actions. Alexander of Aphrodisias was perhaps drawing on Chrysippus when he gave this as a Stoic argument:

If those things are attributable to us of which we can do the opposite, and if praise, blame, encouragement and discouragement, penalties and honours attach to such things, then to be wise and to possess virtues will not be attributable to those who possess them, because they are not capable of having the opposite vices; similarly the vices will not be attributable to wicked men, for it is not in their power to cease being wicked. But it is very odd to deny that our virtues and vices are attributable to us, and to say that we should not be praised or blamed for them (*De Fata*, c. 26).

Chrysippus was concerned to support not free will but moral responsibility. In a sense man's actions are in his power, since he can do them, but it is not in his power not to do them. Yet he is to be praised for acting rightly and blamed if he acts wrongly.

This is a position that many people find it impossible to accept, feeling that if a man's character and actions are finally determined by Fate, he cannot be held responsible for them, that is to say he is not morally responsible and cannot be blamed for them. Yet although there were Greeks who took this view of the problem, it was by no means universally held. The chorus in Aeschylus' *Agamemnon* speaks of Zeus 'responsible for all things, worker of all things' and ask 'what of these happenings was not ordained by the gods?' (1485-8), but a few lines later demand of Clytaemnestra 'who will testify that you are not responsible for this murder?' A similar attitude was required of the Stoic. The fact that he could not help acting as he did in no way diminished the fact that it was he who so acted.

Critics of the Stoic scheme asked why we should give people advice, reproof, exhortation and punishment, if their actions were pre-determined. This was a particular case of a more general argument, known as the Argument for Inaction. If future events are already determined, they will occur whatever one does; it is therefore unnecessary to do anything. As an illustration opponents of Stoicism argued as follows. If it is fated that you will recover from your disease, you will recover whether you call in a doctor or not; there is therefore no point in calling in a doctor. Chrysippus replied that many events are necessarily associated with other events; for example, the birth of a child cannot occur wthout the previous intercourse of its parents. If the birth is fated, the intercourse must be fated along with it. Similarly recovery from a disease may be impossible without medical help. So, if your recovery is fated, it must also be fated that you call in a doctor.

Fate then, is the ultimate cause of all wickedness, and Fate is also Providence, at least in Chrysippus' eyes. Cleanthes is reported to have held that some things that were fated were not providential, but this was never orthodox. How can a good God be the cause of evil? Chrysippus attempted a justification in the fourth book of his work *On Providence*:

> Nothing is more foolish than the opinion of those persons who think that there could have been good things without there being bad things at the same time. Since good things and bad are opposites, they must be set against one another and as it were buttress one another. Of two opposites neither exists without the other. How could there be any conception of justice unless it is an absence of injustice? How could bravery be understood except by the juxtaposition of cowardice, or self-control except by that of licence? How could there be good sense without folly? Why do these foolish men not demand that there should be truth and no falsehood?

This argument rests on the principle that if there are two opposites, both must exist. Hence there must be bad things, if there are to be good. The existence of good things is to be desired, and cannot be realised without bad.

An *ad hominem* reply to this would be as follows: you, Chrysippus, say that there are no good men and therefore no good actions in the contemporary world; any good men there have been lived in the past. Hence good and bad need not exist simultaneously, the principle of coexistence of opposites would be satisfied if there had been one bad man in the past and all men today were good. Why is the world not arranged like that, but the other way round: a multitude of real bad men, balanced by a few dead good ones? Is this providential? But more generally the principle of the coexistence of opposites needs examination. Chrysippus was right in saying that there cannot be truth without there being falsehood; but that does not mean that there cannot be a man who believes a particular truth unless there is another who believes the corresponding falsehood. The truth that $2+2=4$ implies the falsehood of $2+2=5$; it does not imply that anyone entertains that false proposition. Similarly in one sense justice implies injustice; if you know what justice is, you also know what injustice is.

But the fact that some men are just or brave does not in itself imply that there are others who are unjust or cowardly. There is no logical reason why all men should not be virtuous, any more than there is any logical reason why they should not all be healthy or musically gifted.

But is there some practical reason? If virtue depends on right thinking, or the correct use of reason, which is not formed before the age of fourteen and which after its formation requires long exercise before it can be used correctly, every man must be bad before he can be good. Even if this is true of human reason as it is, why on Stoic principles should it be necessary for reason to function incorrectly at all? The explanation given was that the child inevitably accepted certain falsehoods as true. From the first he liked pleasure and disliked pain; this lured him into falsely believing the former to be good, the latter bad. He was also surrounded by elders who were always praising riches, glory, and so on as good and condemning their opposites as bad. He inevitably accepted these current opinions, and so his reason operated from false premises, and was therefore necessarily perverted. Even as an account of what in fact happens this is inadequate, because children brought up in the same environment show very differing degrees of perversion; it will not serve as a defence of Providence, since it does not explain why the general run of popular opinion is so wrong; if a few men can arrive at the truth, why cannot all? Some Stoics said that Providence was not to be blamed: Providence gave men reason, a necessary tool if they were to become good, but reason could also be used for bad ends. Given to be used well, it could be perverted to commit crimes. Here is an attempt to ascribe autonomous action to the human being: he does what he wants, not what God wants. But this, as has been seen, is not a position that could be occupied by a Stoic if he were to remain consistent with his other doctrines. Even if it is allowed, there is another difficulty, put by Cicero's Cotta, when he addresses God as follows: 'You say that the fault lies in man's defects; you should have given them a type of reason that excluded defect and fault.' (*Nature of the Gods* 3. 76.)

It was easier to explain the existence of what are normally called evils, but were not given that name by the Stoics, since they were not morally evil. Chrysippus could see in natural disasters the hand of God, punishing the wicked. Plutarch reports that he quoted Hesiod,

On them from Heav'n Cronus' son drove a great calamity,
A famine and a plague: and the people perish.

and said that the gods do this so that when the bad men are punished, the others will see them as examples and be less inclined to act in their manner. Throughout the ages this has been a popular explanation of natural calamities in a world supposed to be divinely ruled: yet there is no evidence that famine hits the wicked more than the innocent, and in fact since they will hoard and steal they probably suffer less. Chrysippus could have argued that while the hunger of the guilty is a punishment and a warning, that of the innocent serves another purpose, providing them with an opportunity of acting as they should, with patience, self-sacrifice, and acceptance of their fate. He is not known to have made this defence, but it would fit other statements to the effect that things apparently disadvantageous were intended as a stimulus to virtue. Destructive wild animals served the purpose of stimulating bravery among the hunters. Even mice and bed-bugs had their use, the former to encourage tidiness and the latter to discourage slothful lying abed.

War, said Chrysippus, checked over-population; and it could indeed be argued that it was the lesser evil of the two. But there is a criticism near to hand. Given over-population, a war or a plague might serve a purpose, but why should a benevolent God have caused these excessive births in the first place?

The sufferings which sometimes afflicted men who were innocent according to ordinary ways of thought were something of an embarrassment; there is a natural repugnance to attributing them to Providence. Perhaps the most satisfactory answer was to be given by Seneca. After quoting a saying of his contemporary Demetrius, a Cynic: 'No one seems to me more miserable than the man who has not been touched by adversity' he continued: 'indeed he has not been allowed to test himself; if everything has gone as he could wish or even better than he wished, the gods have had a low opinion of him; he has not been thought to deserve an occasional victory over ill-fortune . . . God hardens, examines and trains those he loves . . . Why does God visit bad health and loss of those dear to them and other troubles on the best of mankind? Because in the army the most dangerous tasks are assigned to the bravest soldiers . . . No one who goes out on a dangerous mission says "the commander has treated me badly" but "he has judged me well". In the same way those who are ordered to suffer what would cause the fearful and cowardly to weep should say, "God has found us worthy men on whom to try what human nature can bear".' (*On Providence* IV.)

It is unfortunate that Chrysippus did not confine himself to this line. On some occasion he suggested that the government of the world might be like that of a large household, where trifles may be overlooked, and on another that there were evil demons, whose function was to punish the wicked, but who might get out of hand to afflict the innocent. Such ideas, based on popular concepts, are plainly inconsistent with fundamental Stoic views, and should be regarded as aberrations rather than integral parts of his philosophy. Yet it was a weakness in Chrysippus that he grasped thus readily at handy excuses without facing their implications.

7

Personalities of the Earlier Stoa

In this chapter an attempt is made to characterise the leading figures of the so-called Old Stoa, relating them if possible to the society in which they lived. One interesting problem, which unfortunately admits of no clear answer, is the financial position of teachers and pupils. The latter probably included some poor men as well as prosperous ones; the satirist Timon spoke of 'dirty naked creatures' among Zeno's following and it may be guessed their condition was due to poverty rather than choice. Certainly Cleanthes was without means and when he became head of the school, he must have been supported by gifts from his admirers or fees from his pupils. Chrysippus too is said to have taken fees. There is nothing to show whether the same was true of his successors. Panaetius and Posidonius are the first eminent Stoics known to have been rich men.

Although the columns erected at the expense of the Athenian state to honour the dead Zeno testified to his good influence on the young, who must have been predominantly Athenians, his recorded pupils all came from other cities, evidence of the attraction of Athens as an intellectual centre. They included Aristo from Chios, whose simplified version of his master's teaching has been mentioned (p. 38); Herillus from Carthage, who is said to have been a brief but powerful writer, critical of Zeno[1]; Dionysius from Heraclea on the Black Sea, a poet, who became notorious because when severe ophthalmia convinced him that it was wrong to deny pain to be an evil, he abandoned Stoicism in favour of hedonism; Persaeus from Citium, Philonides from Thebes, Sphaerus from the Bosporus, all men who went to the courts of kings (see p. 140); Callippus from Corinth, Posidonius from Alexandria, Athenodorus from Soli, Zeno from Sidon.

More important than any of these was Cleanthes, who came from Assos some 30 miles south of Troy. It was a town where

[1] His view that the end to be pursued was knowledge is unsympathetically reported, and cannot be profitably discussed.

the Platonists Erastus and Coriscus had worked and Aristotle had spent two years. Cleanthes laboured by night as a drawer of water to support himself and to be free to hear Zeno by day. Although he is said to have had a slow mind, and the fragments suggest a lack of philosophical acuteness, he had merits which explain why Zeno chose him as his successor. He was sincere in his devotion to the new doctrines and he wrote easily in a pleasing and simple way. His ethical teaching was illustrated by vivid similes and instances, as when, to attack the Epicureans, he would tell his audience to imagine a painting where Pleasure sat on a throne beautifully clad and carrying the insignia of royalty; the Virtues were at her side as serving-maids, with no other duties than to minister to her and whisper in her ear that she should avoid any imprudent act which might give offence or be the source of pain: 'We Virtues were born to be your slaves; that is our only function.'

Nine of the fragments—almost the only ones to preserve his own wording—are in competent verse, a form which can make memorable and attractive the thoughts expressed. It may be guessed that passages in metre were inserted into his prose works (cf. Seneca, *Letters* 108. 9–10). He said that although philosophic thought could sufficiently explain things divine as well as human, prose did not possess phrases to go with divine greatness; but metre and tune and rhythm matched the truth to be found in the consideration of the divine. His famous *Hymn to Zeus* expresses the exaltation he felt as he recognised God's omnipotence and his own kinship to this marvellous power:

> Of Gods most glorious, known by many names,
> Power supreme, O Lord of Nature's changes,
> Law-giving pilot of the Universe,
> I hail Thee, Zeus, with whom there is no man
> Forbidden converse: we are of Thy race;
> Of all the beasts that live and walk the earth
> Only we have a semblance of Thy Reason:
> So shall I ever hymn Thee and Thy power.
>
> This ordered Universe, wheeling round Earth,
> Obeys Thee, whereso-e'er Thou dost lead it,

Thy willing subject: such is the tool
Of Thy unconquered hand, the double-edged
Firm flash of the ever-living lightning,
Beneath whose stroke all Nature takes its course.
Thereby Thou dost direct that common plan
That finds its way through all things, with the lamps
Of Heaven mingled, great and small alike;
Thereby Thou art so great, thereby supreme,
Eternal, universal King. No deed
On earth is done apart from Thee, O God,
Nor in the aetherial Heaven, nor the sea,
Save only what the folly of evil men
Self-taught performs. But yet Thy skill it is
To make the crooked straight, disorder order;
To Thee unwelcome things are welcome yet;
All good and evil Thou hast joined to make
One whole, one plan, eternal and complete.
All wicked men lead lives in flight from it,
Wretches, who hunger after acquisition
Of things thought good, and have not eyes nor ears
For God's one Law, obedience to which
As sense dictates would give them happy life.
But senseless, each to his own ill, they rush;
Some pursue glory by the road of strife,
Others are turned to gain without restraint,
And some relax in sensual delights,
But all win evil, turn they here or there
In thwarted eagerness to find the good.

O Zeus, all-bountiful, whose dazzling lightning
Splits Thy black clouds, rescue mankind from wretched
Ignorance, scatter darkness from their minds,
Give them that wisdom by which Thou dost steer
All things in justice; for so honoured, we
Shall honour with honour repay, lauding Thy works
Unceasingly, as mortals fitly do,
Since greater glory has no man, no god,
Than due praise of the Universal Law.

Cleanthes is often criticised for being 'grossly material'. This is unfair. Stoicism is a materialist philosophy and he was right to try to explain things in material terms. His weakness was that his explanations were naïve, as when he understood a presentation to be a three-dimensional reproduction in the *psyche* of a three-dimensional physical object. He had a penchant for arbitrary statements that recall the methods of pre-Socratics: he could declare the stars to be conical and the moon to be shaped like a hat, or detail the stages of the world-conflagration and its quenching. When Aristarchus suggested that the sun, not the earth, was at the centre of things, his reply was not to criticise his mathematics but to say that he should be put on trial for impiety, for having attempted to move 'the hearth stone of the world'.

The invention or development of the idea of tension (p. 76), a force that not only maintains the world as a whole but also gives strength to individual bodies and individual souls, was his chief contribution to Stoic theory.

Chrysippus, who succeeded Cleanthes and (we are told) frequently differed from him, was a native of Soli in Cilicia, where his father had moved from Tarsus. In Soli the Greek language was mangled by non-Greek inhabitants, as a result of which syntactical errors came to be known as 'sclecisms'. Galen suggests that Greek was not Chrysippus' native tongue and the extracts preserved from his books prove that he wrote it always inelegantly and sometimes incorrectly There is nothing to show why he came to Athens or why he took to philosophy, unless credence can be given to Hecato's story that this was due to the confiscation of his father's property. But he began in the Academy, working with the sceptics Arcesilaus and Lacydes, before becoming a pupil of Cleanthes. The simple life that he later led may have been due to choice rather than necessity. He adopted a regular routine which enabled him to produce his great output of books as well as lecturing, probably not in the Stoa but in the Odeum or concert-hall below the acropolis, in the Lyceum, which was a public place of exercise, and in the country at Zoster.

His style was copious and repetitive, and he included generous quotations from other authors, Homer and the tragedians, to illustrate his opinions, so that someone once, when asked what book he was reading, replied 'Chrysippus' *Medea*.[1] His writings on psychology, the chief source of fragments, were remarkably clumsy and ill-constructed. The following is not an unfair sample or unfair rendering:

> The sense in which one speaks of excess of impulse is because it goes beyond the natural due proportion of the impulses in relation to the men themselves. What I mean might be more intelligible as follows. To take an example, in the case of walking associated with an impulse, the movement of the legs is not excessive but ceases more or less simultaneously with the impulse, so as to change and come to a standstill when one wants. But in the case of those who run in association with an impulse nothing of the sort happens, but the movement of the legs is excessive in comparison with the impulse, so that it is carried away and does not change obediently like that as soon as they put it in hand. I imagine that something parallel happens in the case of the impulses as a consequence of their going beyond the due proportion which accords with reason, so that when there is an impulse it is not obediently disposed, the excess in the case of running being understood as going beyond the impulse and in the case of an impulse as going beyond reason. The due proportion of a natural impulse is that which agrees with reason, going so far and so long as reason itself requires. And so, as the over-run takes place in this respect and in this manner, it is said that there is 'an excessive impulse' and 'an unnatural irrational movement of the *psyche*' (quoted by Galen, *Views of Hippocrates and Plato*, 4. p. 338 M).

Extracts from his works on ethics show a somewhat less turgid manner of writing. The following seems to indicate a view that a philosopher's primary concern is with the improvement of his fellow-men:

> Those who suppose that the scholarly life is most appropriate for philosophers seem to me to be wrong from the start, as

[1] He is known to have quoted Euripides' play in his long work *On the Passions*.

assuming that they should do this for the sake of entertainment of sorts or something of that kind and that they should spin out their whole life in that way, which is, if looked at clearly, pleasantly. Their assumption should not go unnoticed, many making it explicitly, but not a few doing it more obscurely (quoted by Plutarch, *Moralia* 1033 D).

The following, from his book *On Appropriate Action*, is one of a number of passages which show him to have maintained the tradition of the Cynics in challenging accepted conventions:

When our parents have left us, the simplest form of burial should be used, on the view that the body means nothing to us, any more than do the nails, teeth, or hair, and that we have no need of any such care or consideration. So, if their flesh is useful, they will use it for food, just as if of one's own limbs the foot, shall we say, were amputated it would be right to use it, and so on. But if the flesh is useless, they will either bury it and forget it, or burn it and scatter the ashes, or throw it right away, paying it no more attention than a nail or hair (quoted by Sextus, *Against the Dogmatists* 11.194, *Outlines of Pyrrhonism* 3.248; there are slight differences of wording between his two versions).

Probably, like Zeno in his *Republic*, Chrysippus was here laying down rules of conduct for an ideal society, not suggesting that they should be followed in contemporary Greece.

The common opinion that he was the source of orthodox Stoicism is probably correct, although it is possible that much of the systematisation found in later authors was not his work. The defects of his style left a place for shorter and clearer versions, and it is a likely guess that these were supplied by his successors, whose works are often cited by Diogenes Laertius alongside his, even for the most basic doctrines. It is also easy to understand that later teachers found it useful to expound his writings to their pupils, as Epictetus did, although at the same time he upbraided those who thought philosophy a matter of reading Chrysippus, not of learning how to live. But to read him had much to offer for those with patience. He was very ready to think of difficulties to which Stoic doctrines might give rise and to attempt to deal with them; he is said frequently to have corrected himself, but sometimes to have confessed himself beaten.

Chrysippus' successor as head of the School, Zeno of Tarsus, had many pupils but nothing original to contribute. He was followed by a more important figure, Diogenes, who came from Seleucia, the new Greek city alongside old Babylon, whence he was known as 'Diogenes of Babylon'. Possessed of a clear, simple style, he was able to hand on the work of his predecessors in a palatable form, sometimes restating arguments to avoid possible criticisms. He is known to have written on grammar, on the seat of the intelligence, on theology, where he followed Cleanthes and Chrysippus in explaining the gods of mythology as personified aspects of the one god who ruled the universe,[1] and on ethics (see p. 55). His views on music and rhetoric were attacked by the Epicurean Philodemus, and the discovery at Herculaneum of large fragments of the latter's works has preserved much information about them. To all intents he is the sole surviving authority for Stoic views on these subjects, and it is impossible to say how far he was here an original thinker.

Rhetoric, as it was practised in his time, he thought to be useless; orators (or politicians as we should call them) were unable to influence individuals to manage their private lives well, and this suggested that their effect on public life would be equally unhelpful; there was hardly a known instance of an orator's having deserved well of his city as an ambassador; the orator, *qua* orator, had not the necessary knowledge to benefit his city; that he could only get from philosophy. Orators were

[1]Like his predecessors he made much use of 'etymology', or the supposed discovery in a word of allusions to other words relevant to its meaning. Thus he saw in *Athe*na Zeus' power extending into the *aithe*r. A work by a Stoic of the first century AD, Cornutus, teacher of the poet Persius, still survives, which explains the Olympians as symbols for parts of or processes in the natural world: e.g. *Heph*aestus is the fire we use, so-called because of its being lighted (*heph*thai). The influence of this sort of thinking, strange and unacceptable to us, although not altogether disparaged by Plato, extended outside the Stoic school.

trained in methods of deceit and could use it for bad purposes. Yet laymen sometimes had the better of them by speaking the plain truth; the Spartans had no use for rhetoric, but got their own way; even the Athenians, with their love for orators, were becoming critical of their technique and their periods. Yet he recognised that there was a proper art of rhetoric and virtues of style to be used by the man who knew the correct ends of persuasion. These virtues were good Greek, clarity, concision, appropriateness of language to the occasion, and technical elaboration. What exactly he meant by the last phrase must be uncertain: he defined it as 'getting away from the language of the man-in-the-street'.

His views about music are reminiscent of those of Plato and, like him, he appealed to the authority of the musician Damon. Music displayed character and could affect the characters of those who heard it; it could be magnificent or humble, manly or womanly, orderly or arrogant. It had a place in the culture of all peoples; its use in religious ceremonies was notable; it helped to control the passions of love and of grief; it could encourage the manual worker. The addition of music to the words of a poem increased its effect on the mind. Music promoted the kind of drinking-party that could be approved: 'no form of play and relaxation is more suitable for free men than that one should sing, another play the *cithara*,[1] another dance; and love is better when accompanied by vocal music, not that of the pipe'. Some Stoics may have deserved their modern reputation for stern sobriety, but this passage is a reminder that at this time at least they could unhesitatingly accept some normal and harmless pleasures.

Philodemus' criticisms of Diogenes are sometimes captious, but he made the effective point that there was no evidence that the songs of Ibycus, Anacreon, and Agathon had, as Diogenes had assumed, been a bad influence on the young, or, if they had been, that the music was responsible, not the words.

The most significant event in Diogenes' life was his visit to Rome. In 155 BC he was sent there as an octogenarian on an embassy along with Carneades, head of the Academy, who had once been his pupil in logic, and Critolaus, head of the Peripa-

[1] A stringed instrument, played by plucking.

tetics, to appeal against a decision given by the Sicyonians acting as arbitrators; they had condemned Athens to pay the heavy fine of 500 talents to the neighbouring state of Oropus. Greece was still nominally independent, but the Roman Senate was not averse to using pressure to influence its affairs. The choice of these philosophers was doubtless due to their having a reputation outside Athens; this and the honesty which they might be supposed to practise would perhaps recommend Athens' case better than the suspect characters of obscure politicians.[1] While in Rome all three men lectured on philosophical topics, a novelty in that city, and attracted much attention. Carneades had something of a *succès-de-scandale* by defending and attacking the concept of justice on successive days, but Diogenes impressed by his sensible morality. He was the first Stoic teacher to visit Rome, and the first of a long line.

Antipater of Tarsus, a contemporary of Carneades, defended the Stoic position against his attacks by means of numerous books, which were read along with those of Chrysippus two hundred years later. It is possible that his formulations are to be seen in some of the later accounts. He was an influential champion but not an important innovator; innovation was to come from his pupil and admirer Panaetius. To us he is interesting because he is the first Stoic from whom there survive examples of the practical advice that philosophers found it more and more their business to give. They are written in an eloquent although easy-going style, very unlike that of Chrysippus. His advice to a man in search of a wife reads a little absurdly today, but was sensible in a society where the suitor had little opportunity of getting to know his bride-to-be. The man was not to look for wealth or good birth or any other vanity, let alone beauty, which always creates a proud and despotic character: he must look into her father's character and her mother's; then, if they are good, see if they have brought the girl up to be like themselves or spoiled her through excessive fondness; he should inquire into this in various ways, from slaves and free men, from members of the

[1]That Stoics were now playing a part in civic life at Athens is shown by an inscription probably of 151/150 which includes several men known to be Stoics among the officials at the festival Ptolemaea (IG II² 1938).

household, from neighbours and friends, from cooks and work-men and workwomen who have been in the house; people are all too ready to trust such persons with information they should not have.

A long passage on marriage attacks those who selfishly remain single, and points out that they not only fail in a duty but also miss a blessing.

A man with no experience of a wife and children has not tasted the truest and most genuine kind of goodwill. Other kinds of friendship and affection are like the mixing by juxta-position of beans or the like, but the affection of a man and wife resembles the complete blending of wine and water. For they alone share not only their property and their children, man's dearest possession, and their souls, but their very bodies also (Stobaeus 4.67.25).

The wife will of course be subordinate to her husband; that she should be expected to support his political or intellectual life without sharing it was inevitable in the social circumstances of the time. But husband and wife were to form a partnership: 'if one should take a second self as it were (and it makes no dif-ference whether male or female), one would do all one's work much more lightly and easily.'

The views and historical importance of Panaetius, Antipater's successor, are treated in other chapters (pp. 123 and 142). A member of a leading family in Rhodes, he came to Athens as a young man to study philosophy. He was probably in his late thirties when the younger Scipio, the conqueror of Carthage, some ten years his senior, took him as a friend on an embassy to Egypt in 140 BC, and it is likely that they had made one another's acquaintance in Rome. He certainly spent consid-erable periods there in the following decade. Before Antipater's death in 129 he was assisting in the teaching at Athens, where he may be supposed to have resided in the main thereafter. At some time he was offered Athenian citizenship, but refused it, on what grounds is not known; the reason he gave, that one city was enough for a man of moderation, was clearly no more than a polite excuse. Such considerations had not deterred Chrysippus from enrolling in the citizen body.

PERSONALITIES OF THE EARLIER STOA

It is a striking fact that down to Panaetius no man of Athenian birth was head of the Stoic school and indeed no Stoic whose views or activities are recorded was an Athenian. But his joint successors, Dardanus and Mnesarchus, were both native Athenians, as was his pupil Apollodorus, who won some reputation as a literary critic. The other schools were predominantly but not exclusively headed by men from abroad, except that the Epicurean remained wholly under Athenians. One can only guess at reasons for this. It is possible that the Epicureans found it convenient that their head should as an Athenian citizen be legally capable of owning the Garden together with its buildings where they met. Native Athenians were not so numerous that one would expect them to produce many philosophers of parts, and it may be no more than chance that none adopted Stoicism. Yet there was a factor which may have drawn an Athenian to other schools. If he wished to take part in public affairs, as his citizenship made possible, they offered him a training in rhetoric, or the art of persuasive speech. This was practised both in the Peripatos and in the Academy, where the exercise of speaking on both sides of a question provided a good training. At the end of the second century the Academic Philo of Larisa taught his pupils even how to handle particular cases in the courts, but he represents only the climax of a movement to educate men in rhetoric controlled by philosophy. The Stoics too regarded rhetoric as part of philosophy; it was a division of 'logic'. But for them it was the art of speaking, not persuasively, but truthfully; hence a speaker would find it an inadequate tool to win the votes of a jury or an assembly. There may therefore be some connexion between the nature of Stoic teaching and the absence of prominent Athenian pupils. Now although Panaetius did not, so far as is known, teach a practical art of rhetoric, he certainly encouraged those who were fitted for public life to take part in it, and Cicero reports that he allowed the advocate to defend a man whom he knew to be guilty (*On Duties* 2.51). His teaching may accordingly have been more attractive than that of his predecessors to men who intended to take part in the public life of their city.

Archedemus, who was roughly a contemporary of Panaetius, came from Tarsus; it was a town where learning and philosophy were greatly favoured (Strabo 14.5.13). After studying in Athens he moved to Babylon, or perhaps the twin-town of Seleucia, and there established a school. His writings were later read along with those of Chrysippus and Antipater. His career serves to show that some Stoics regarded philosophy not as a search for truth, which could have been carried on better in Athens, but as its propagation. It may be guessed that there were other less prominent teachers who carried the message to the Greeks and the hellenised Asiatics of other towns in the East.

Nothing is known of where Boethus of Sidon worked. He wrote a commentary in four volumes on the *Weatherlore* of the third-century poet Aratus, a man himself affected by Stoic pantheism. He did not suppose that the sign caused the weather that followed it, but tried to find some single common cause for both. This rationalism appeared also in his rejection of the doctrine that the world would end in a conflagration. He argued first that there was no internal cause to destroy it—a criticism that seems to disregard the orthodox view that fire will eat up all the other elements, until everything is fire. Secondly he maintained that there are three ways in which a thing can be destroyed, by being broken up, by removal of its predominant quality, or by being compounded into something new. The world could not break up; its quality could not be completely removed, since even the supporters of the conflagration said that the quality of the world-order was then concentrated on Zeus; and it could not be compounded, because the four elements would all disappear at once if compounded. As reported, these arguments have little weight; it is a mere assertion that the world cannot break up or that its quality is irremovable. Boethus also asked what God would do after the world had turned to fire; with nothing to look after he would be left in a state of intolerable idleness.

Although he was not a Stoic, Antiochus of Ascalon, who worked in the early part of the first century BC, deserves a mention here. Becoming head of the Academy, he felt that scepticism had had its day. His predecessor, Philo of Larisa, had already admitted that some things could be known, although he had continued to deny that there was any such thing as the 'cognitive presentation' in which the Stoics found the mark of truth. Antiochus abandoned scepticism completely, admitting that there were such presentations and that they were the only road to knowledge.[1] He also ceded to Chrysippus that action is impossible without prior assent to a presentation; Carneades had denied this, since otherwise the sceptic would have been condemned, if he were to live up to his theories, to absolute immobility. 'Cognitive presentations' were therefore necessary. The only difference between the Stoics and Antiochus was that the latter was not satisfied that such presentations could be immediately recognised, but said that before accepting them one should take precautions against error and confirm the health of one's sense-organs. This divergence looked less important than it was.

The most influential part of Antiochus' teaching lay in his historical theory that both Stoicism and Peripateticism were adaptations of Platonism: Zeno had done little more than change the vocabulary, and Aristotle had in ethics been a true follower of Plato, although Theophrastus had regrettably abandoned the position that virtue was of itself enough to bring happiness. A lack of interest in metaphysics[2] and perhaps ignorance, certainly neglect, of the greater part of the writings that form the Aristotelian Corpus made easier this exaggeration of a kernel of truth. Antiochus propounded a system of ethics which he represented as being a modernised version of that of the old Academy, and which he strongly contrasted with the innovations of Zeno, but in practice he borrowed freely from the Stoics. He adopted their account of *oikeiôsis*, the process by which the living being becomes attached to all that accords with its nature, proceeding from the 'primary natural things' to the development of morality under the guidance of reason. But he criticised Zeno for failing to understand that man's 'nature' is physical as well as mental and denying that bodily excellence was to be called good. Zeno had also been wrong in thinking that it was enough to choose rightly among those things that he

[1]There is plenty of evidence for the survival of Carneadean scepticism after Antiochus. The history of the Academy at Athens in the next 100 years is a blank, and its leading members may have reverted to probabilism.

[2]It is disputed whether Antiochus accepted Plato's transcendent Forms. I tend to agree with R. E. Witt, Albinus 57 f. and C. J. de Vogel, *Greek Philosophy* III 278 f. against G. Luck, *Antiochus* 28 ff., that he did not.

called 'indifferent'; *possession* of what is 'primarily natural' must be a factor in happiness. Yet Antiochus regarded it as a minimal factor, which could do no more than slightly increase the happiness that was the gift of virtue. He was entirely at one with the Stoa in lauding the self-sufficiency of the wise and therefore virtuous man.

'With a very few changes, Antiochus would be an absolutely genuine Stoic'; that is a remark made by a character in one of the Dialogues of Cicero (*Academica Priora* 2.132), who was at times much influenced by him. But it is an exaggeration, even when it has been added that Antiochus followed the Stoics in demanding the complete absence of passions. He was keenly aware of the difference which separated him from them. But he is a significant figure in that he suggested that there was much common ground between the various schools of philosophy, and showed that one who was not a Stoic could usefully borrow from those who were. It was to become a feature of the succeeding centuries that Stoic influence became widespread in writers who did not belong to that school, or who were hostile to it.

8

Innovation: Panaetius and Posidonius

PANAETIUS

After Chrysippus the heads of the school down to Antipater
had been champions of orthodoxy. With Panaetius innovation
appears. As the friend of Scipio and other eminent Romans he
had seen wider horizons than was usual for the professional
philosophers who had preceded him. Perhaps this led to his
practical approach: he gave up the inessential and encumbering
doctrine of the world-conflagration, and in his work *On Providence* was sceptical about the reality of prophecy, and in particular utterly rejected the claims of astrology.[1] Probably he did
not write a great deal; his known work was predominantly
ethical and addressed to the problems of conduct that life provided. One book was on political action, another on cheerful-
ness or being of good heart, while that of which we know most
was *On Appropriate Actions*. We owe this entirely to Cicero,
who adapted it for his *De Officiis* or *On Duties*, in such a way
that the outlines of Panaetius' treatment are still visible, and
may be traced as follows.[2]

All animals have a natural tendency to self-preservation, and
to mate for the sake of propagation, and to have some care for
their offspring. Man is distinguished by his possession of reason,

[1]Cicero, *On Divination* 2.85–97. Diogenes of Babylon had already
denied that the stars could foretell the incidents of man's life, but
allowed that they might indicate his character and capabilities. The
conflagration had been rejected by Boethus of Sidon.

[2]More elaborate reconstructions have been made, but although
they include some probable elements, a measure of reserve towards
them will be prudent. Attempts to find evidence for Panaetius in
other works of Cicero are inconclusive. *Talks at Tusculum* 2 has been
supposed to represent a letter by him to Q. Tubero; this seems
unlikely. Some influence in *On Laws* 1 and *On the Republic*, of which
only fragments survive, is probable but its extent cannot be determined. Influence on *On the Nature of the Gods* and *On Friendship*
26–32 is not out of the question, but quite speculative.

which enables him to take a longer and wider view; it increases his love for his children and causes him to develop his co-operative relationship with other men. It is also a mark of man that he wants to learn and know the truth. Along with this goes a desire to be pre-eminent and an unwillingess to take orders except for his own good. Finally man is the only animal with a sense of order and propriety, which makes him appreciate beauty both of the physical world and of an orderly life. From these roots spring the four cardinal virtues; although all are connected, each has its own field.

1. Wisdom, distinguished from the three others by being theoretical and not a practical virtue, consists in knowing the truth. There are two faults in this field; one is false belief that we know what we do not know or hasty acceptance of ideas, the other is to waste effort over difficult and unnecessary subjects. Cicero, who prefers a life of action to one of thought, treats wisdom superficially. It is possible that Panaetius distinguished, as with the other virtues, two aspects, a negative and a positive, which would correspond to the two faults. On the one hand false opinions and unwarranted confidence were to be avoided, on the other one ought to prosecute study of subjects of importance. What these may have been and what he regarded as difficult and unnecessary, can only be guessed. He himself had some interest in the history of philosophy and of philosophers and their writings. He is said to have started his teaching with physics, but there is no evidence that he went beyond generalities to investigate the details of the world of nature, or that he concerned himself with logic. But there is no reason to suppose that he thought everyone should pursue all the branches of learning that could be approved. His emphasis on the capacities of the individual (see below) would tell the other way.

2. Justice is the virtue that arises from the social instincts. Negatively it forbids one man to injure another, to take his private property, or to lay hands on what belongs to the community; positively it is an active beneficence, which forms the bond of society. Cicero develops this theme at length, probably finding much of his material in Panaetius. It is likely enough that the latter insisted that beneficence should be prudently applied, should not exceed the benefactor's means, and should be fitted to the recipient's merits; also that we belong to a num-

ber of communities of different size, the largest being that of the human race, the smallest that of the family. Our positive obligations towards the members of these communities vary, but the firmest link of all is that which binds good men together.

3. Bravery, springing from the desire for pre-eminence, again has two sides, one a disdain for the outer world, a refusal to submit to any other man, to any passion, or to any blow of fortune, and the other a wish to do great and useful deeds that are difficult and dangerous. Bravery is for Panaetius freedom not merely from fear, but also from cupidity; it means too that one will not be tempted by pleasure, moved by pain, or disturbed by anger. Undistracted therefore and undeterred, the brave man, driven on by his selfless ambition, will devote himself to his chosen enterprise. The undertaking that has most interest for Cicero is that of political life, but it must not be assumed that Panaetius gave it the same emphasis. Yet it would not be surprising if he did, in view of his association with some of the leading men at Rome.

It has been suggested that Panaetius preferred to call this virtue greatness of spirit, the quality that Aristotle had regarded as the consummation of the moral virtues. The term 'greatness of spirit' became commonly used among the Romans, often in contexts where one would expect a word for 'bravery'. The initiative for this use may have come from Panaetius, although there is no proof.

4. The fourth cardinal virtue was in Greek called *sophrosyne,* a word for which there is notoriously no English equivalent, unless we can say that its possessor is the man who 'keeps his head'. But the Greeks themselves found the word easier to use than to explain. Panaetius thought that it was closely associated with the notion of 'propriety' (*to prepon,* Latin *decorum*). Propriety demands that appetites should be controlled by reason; it is improper, that is contrary to what we expect from a man who is, unlike a brute beast, a rational being, for them to be out of hand. Again it is improper for a man to be devoted to bodily pleasures, for nature has equipped him to think and to act.

But we have not only the character of being human, each of us is an individual with his own qualities. Propriety requires therefore regard not only for general human nature but also for our own capacities; only thus will a man be able to live a consistent life, and avoid the absurdity of attempting the impossible. But these are not the only considerations for determining propriety of conduct: it must be affected by the position in which fortune has placed us and also by the kind of life we have chosen to lead; this choice of career should be determined by examining both our natural capacity and our circumstances.

Cicero proceeds to develop at length the demands of propriety, sketching the behaviour to be expected of young and of old, emphasising the importance of decency in dress and in language, and inculcating a sense of proportion and of occasion. Basically, no doubt, all this rests on Panaetius, although much of the detail may be adjusted to Roman ideas of good behaviour.

Propriety, although the particular concern of *sophrosyne,* is of course not identical with it. The other virtues and the actions that proceed from them are all appropriate to man.

The loss of the writings of earlier Stoics makes it impossible to be sure how much of this well-thought-out scheme is original. Had it not been used by Cicero, nothing would have been known of it. But there are certain features that appear to be novel.

1. All the virtues are derived from what may be called innate instincts. Hence Panaetius described the 'end' of life as 'living in accordance with the starting-points given us by nature'. But clearly the instincts are not in themselves a sufficient guide to action: they may be the motive-force, but they need the direction that is given them by reason. The part played by reason is so central in Stoic ethics that it cannot have been overlooked by Panaetius in his definition. And indeed it is not overlooked, for it is the most important of the starting-points or assets that nature gives to man. Panaetius' originality lies in associating with it a number of tendencies which can be developed and ordered to secure a good life. One of these, the instinct for self-preservation and for propagation, had been used in a similar way by Chrysippus, but Panaetius is the first Stoic we know to have given man a large endowment of natural assets.

2. In orthodox Stoicism the only good man is the perfectly wise man and he alone is possessed of virtue. Panaetius seems not to have denied this, but to have let it fall out of sight. When a young man asked him whether a wise man would fall in love, he replied 'we will not bother about that now: you and I, who are still far from being wise, must not run the risk of falling into

a state so disturbed and uncontrolled'. The imaginary sage ceases to be the sole ideal towards which all men should strive; each man should have his own ideal, suited to his capacity. Panaetius expressed this by the image of a number of archers all aiming at the same target, but at different marks on it; a darts-board would be the modern equivalent.

3. The emphasis on the positive sides of the virtues of justice and bravery made this a philosophy suitable for men who wished to be leaders of public life. Panaetius also insisted at length that it was essential to obtain other men's co-operation if results of importance were to be achieved. It is perhaps not an accident that he came from Rhodes, an island that had maintained its independence and where the aristocrats, under the guise of a democracy, effectively governed with a strong tradition of service and of care for the welfare of the less fortunate. It was certainly no accident that he exerted a strong influence on a number of his aristocratic Roman friends.

Diogenes Laërtius reports that Panaetius and his pupil Posidonius (see p. 129) thought that virtue was not sufficient for happiness, but that one needed health, financial resources, and strength (7.128); elsewhere (7.103) he claims that Posidonius thought riches and health to be good, and that claim is certainly false. It is improbable that Panaetius, even although he greatly admired Aristotle, here went over to the Peripatetic position. One of the best-known distinctions between Peripatos and Stoa was, after all, that the former believed happiness to require the possession of something more than virtue; yet neither Cicero nor any reputable author hints that Panaetius was not orthodox on this central doctrine. Indeed we have seen that it was of the essence of bravery that one should look down on all external things, and that nothing should be admired or wished for but morality. (*On Duties* 1.66.) It may be right to reject Diogenes' evidence as a simple misrepresentation, but if there is anything in it the explanation may be that both Panaetius and Posidonius held that these morally indifferent advantages were necessary pre-conditions of some kinds of virtuous action, not that virtue did not bring happiness without them, but that without them one could not act virtuously in every way. The positive side of Panaetius' virtue of justice will require monetary resources, the positive side of bravery needs health and strength; a poor

THE STOICS

man cannot make public benefactions and a bedridden man cannot engage in the perils of war, exploration, or political life.

Yet Panaetius cannot have meant that a poor man or a sick man cannot be virtuous. He recognised that correct action was not the same for all, but depended on circumstances. He may not have been aware of the difficulties that this would bring for the doctrine that virtue does not admit of degree.

Panaetius made some changes from orthodox Stoic psychology, reducing the parts of the *psyche* to six. He did not maintain a separate element concerned with speech, but assimilated it to other deliberate bodily movements; and he ascribed sexual activity to *physis* (nature), as taking place automatically, like the functions of nutrition and growth. It seems therefore that whereas the orthodox had supposed that the *physis* which ruled the unborn child was entirely converted at birth in to *psyche,* he thought that some at least persisted, to determine what others had seen as being psychical processes.

The most important of Panaetius' Greek pupils were Hecato of Rhodes and the much greater Posidonius. Both rejected much of his teaching. But Hecato wrote at length on 'appropriate action', and busied himself with casuistry, the discussion of cases in which it was difficult to decide what was appropriate. This was not a new departure. Diogenes of Babylon had imagined the situation of a man who brought a cargo of wheat to a town in the grip of famine: ought he to reveal to purchasers his knowledge that several more ships carrying grain were close behind him? Diogenes argued that he was under no obligation to do so and thereby depress the price he could obtain. Antipater on the other hand thought that silence would be immoral. Diogenes believed that one should pass on a false coin that one had received, and sell without remark a thieving slave or wine that had turned sour. We should perhaps side with Antipater who took the other view.

Hecato decided that in a shipwreck a wise man would not snatch a plank from a madman, and that a son should not give information about his father whom he knew to be tunnelling into the public treasury, but that he ought in the last resort to denounce him if he were trying to seize autocratic power. If the price of food were very high, it would be right to let one's slaves starve, but one should not throw them overboard to lighten ship in preference to horses more valuable than they. Discussions of this kind may seem strange activities for philosophers and philosophers may be thought no more equipped than others to solve such moral problems. But the Stoic claimed to be a guide to conduct, not a mere dealer in theory, and he might say that by exercising himself over such questions he had trained his judgment and was more likely than others to give the right answer.

POSIDONIUS

Posidonius, a wealthy man from Apamea in northern Syria, after being a pupil of the aged Panaetius at Athens, made his home in Rhodes, at that time a flourishing intellectual centre. Still an independent state, it had a famous school of rhetoric and had also given refuge to learned exiles from Alexandria. Here he enjoyed citizenship—it can only be guessed how he came to have it—filled the high office of *prytanis*, and in the winter of 87 to 86 BC was sent on an embassy to Rome. His books and his lectures brought him fame, and something of a school grew around him.

Surviving extracts from his writing show him to have matched his style to his subject as he ranged from simple clarity to a powerful and biting manner, marked by a wide vocabulary, striking similes and metaphors, ironic allusions, and play upon words. In using this last arresting style he was the practitioner of a kind of Hellenistic prose about to go out of fashion, but the 'rhetoric' of which he is accused by the geographer Strabo is there not for its own sake, but is expressive of his feelings and attitudes and gives a vivid idea of his personality.

At one time it was fashionable to see Posidonius' influence in almost every subsequent author, and attempts were made to reconstruct Protean philosophies, in which all contradictions were reconciled, from the works of these supposed followers. This excess led to a sceptical reaction. Yet some influence he must have had. Given the partial nature of the evidence, no picture of Posidonius will escape distortion, but one that is based exclusively on attested fragments and doctrines may be unnecessarily distorted and incomplete. To go beyond them is, however, fraught with difficulty. Even if an author names Posidonius as his source, it is hard to know how much has been taken from him; when an author does not name him, but expresses views known to have been his, it need not follow that he was the source even of these, let alone of associated matter; too little is known about Posidonius' predecessors, so that he and the later author may for all we can tell be independently following some earlier model. At present a little unattested material would be accepted by most scholars as Posidonian; in time a little more may be safely added to the picture. In what follows I have tried not to venture far beyond the bounds of certainty.[1]

Posidonius was a man of original, inquiring, and wide-ranging mind with a synoptic vision of the world. If there is one characteristic which stands out, it is the way in which he saw all things as connected. Although this was implicit in traditional Stoicism and Chrysippus had talked of *sympatheia* or sympathetic affection of the parts of the whole, Posidonius gave the idea new emphasis. Typically he modified the old comparison of the parts of philosophy to the wall, the trees, and the fruits of an orchard by comparing them to the interacting parts of an animal, bones and sinews, flesh and blood, and *psyche*. In keeping with this he was unwilling to see sharp divisions in the world; traditionally there were three kingdoms, animal, vegetable, and mineral, the inhabitants of which were organised by different forms of indwelling breath, by *psyche* (life), *physis* (growth) and *hexis* (condition). According to Posidonius a 'life-force' could be recognised everywhere. Man is not sharply cut off from the 'brute' beasts; they too show glimmerings of intelligence, and his *psyche* is not pure reason, but has its vegetative and irrational parts. This is Aristotelian, whether by influence or coincidence; Aristotelian too was his interest in the causes of

[1] I take it as certain that Diodorus Siculus used Posidonius extensively for Books 5 and 34 of his *History*, and that Strabo used him more than he admits. An indeterminate amount of Cleomedes *On Circular Motion* and a small part of Vitruvius *On Architecture* Book VIII admittedly come from the philosopher. Posidonian influence seems probable in Cicero *On the Nature of the Gods* II, 23–32, 49–56, 115–153. Seneca may have made a little more use of him than he notes. Beyond this there is little that is not speculative. Much has been based on the supposition that Nemesius (? fifth century AD) indirectly transmits much from Posidonius; the ground seems to me treacherous.

phenomena, an interest of which Strabo, a more orthodox Stoic, disapproved. Traditionally it had been usual to regard effective causes as obscure and take refuge in a vague ascription of all things to the ultimate cause, God. For Posidonius the discovery of intermediate causation brought proof of how all things worked together. He was not satisfied with generalities; knowledge of the parts was necessary for understanding of the whole. Accordingly, like Aristotle, he thought it valuable to observe and record details in many fields of knowledge. The philosopher ought to care to know how the divine power works. Wisdom had been defined as 'knowledge of divine and human things *and of their causes*'; he put a new emphasis on the words in italics.

This curiosity took him, probably in the first decade of the first century, on one or more journeys to the West, not merely to Rome, but to Sicily, to wild Liguria, and outside the Roman boundaries into Gaul. Several vivid sketches of that rude society survive: the paying of men to allow their throats to be cut for public amusement, the nailing of skulls as trophies to the doorway ('an unfamiliar sight, but one gets used to it'), the huge meals where men gnawed whole joints, like lions. But he took the honour paid to the bards and to the Druids, whom he saw as philosophers, to be a sign that even among the most savage barbarians 'pride and passion give way to wisdom, and Ares stands in awe of the Muses' (Diodorus 5.31).

It was in Spain that he made his most famous observations, on the Atlantic coast at Gades, the modern Cadiz. Here he noticed that the daily ebb and flow of the tide was connected with the circling of the earth by the moon. The people of those parts told him, according to Strabo (3.5.8), of the yearly changes that brought especially high tides at the summer solstice; he said that he spent some days at Gades when the moon was full at that solstice, but was unable to confirm their statement; at the new moon, however, being inland, he was able to observe the effects of what he supposed to be a remarkable high tide: the river Baitis (modern Guadalquivir) was pent up and overflowed. He knew that there was a cycle which brought the highest tides at full and new moon and the least at half-moon. He concluded that there was a similar yearly cycle with peaks at the solstices and lows at the equinoxes. In fact the high tides come at the equinoxes, as was known a century later to Seneca and Pliny.

The guess, commonly made, that they had this from Posidonius and that he was misrepresented by Strabo seems to be rooted in the belief that such a great man cannot have been mistaken or misunderstood his informants.[1]

Probably Posidonius brought to the ignorant dwellers by the almost tideless Mediterranean something well-known to those who lived on the shores of the open sea; but he did all he could to verify the facts, and he tried also to explain them. The explanation was of course inadequate; he seems to have thought that the heat of the moon, which he believed to be a mixture of air and fire, caused a swelling of the water, without being strong enough to evaporate it (why then should there by a high tide at new moon?).[2] But he saw in the connexion of moon and sea evidence of the unifying spirit that integrated the world. This same cosmic sympathy he found illustrated by various tales of connexion between the phases of the moon and the growth of plants and animals.

The work best represented in surviving fragments is his *History* in 52 volumes, which took up the story of the world where Polybius had left off in 145 BC. But his conception is very different. Whereas Polybius was cool and factual, he sees events as caused by human psychology, whether of the individual or of the crowd; he can understand men's passions and follies, but he does not pardon or excuse them. He believes in aristocratic rule and that the Romans deserved their dominance, but fears that moral decay is ruining the order of society. He is therefore emotionally involved in the history he records, using all his skill to enlist the reader's approval or condemnation of the actors.

The brilliance of Posidonius' account of the Sicilian slave-rising of 135–132 BC is still recognisable in Photius' summary of Diodorus' lost book 34. There was a vivid picture of the multitudes of slaves acquired by the great landowners, mostly Roman *equites* but also Sicilian Greeks, and of their brutal treatment.

[1]Priscianus Lydus (sixth century AD) gives the correct view in a passage which begins with an acknowledgment to Posidonius. I see no reason for preferring this evidence to the detailed and coherent account given by Strabo.

[2]This depends on Priscianus Lydus. Aetius gives it as Posidonius' view that the moon caused winds which in turn caused the tides.

Then the owners, to avoid the cost of feeding their shepherds, encouraged them to live by brigandage; the countryside became perilous to travellers and farms were plundered. The slaves, organising themselves in armed bands for their rapine, began to feel their own strength. The Roman praetors who governed the island were intimidated from any firm action because the owners were *equites*, members of the order who formed the juries at Rome and who would try them if they were accused of maladministration. (This last point appears to be an anachronism, since the courts did not fall under the control of the *equites* until 122; it seems most probable that Posidonius confused the situation before the second slave-rising of 103 with that ruling before the first.)

The explosive situation having been thus explained, he went on to show how individuals put the spark to it. The cruelty of Damophilus, an ostentatiously rich Greek of Enna, drove his slaves to desperation, and they received encouragement from a Syrian slave who had set up as a magician and prophet and been used by his master as an entertaining turn at dinner-parties. He had been accustomed to prophesy that he would himself become a king, and now at the head of 400 armed slaves he seized the town of Enna. The story goes on with the spread of the revolt, with the torture and the slaughter of the owners, and with the final bloody suppression of the rebels after the siege of Tauromenium (modern Taormina), where the starving slaves resorted to cannibalism. But Posidonius made it clear that men were not naturally wild beasts; these slaves had been depraved by the cruelty and cupidity of their masters. He noted that Damophilus' daughter, who had succoured her parents' victims, was allowed to go unharmed.[1]

In his accounts of the terrestial globe Posidonius seems to have been a good eye-witness, but uncritical in his theorising. He argued that the earth's 'torrid' zone was not all uninhabitable, but had a cooler central or equatorial strip. Perhaps he had

[1]The longest, very readable, and partially verbatim extract from the *History* concerns one Athenio, who carried the Athenians to the losing side in the Mithridatic war of 88 BC: see Athenaeus 211e–215c. Tarn's complaint, *Hellenistic Civilisation*, p. 286, that he neglected the true causes of anti-Roman feeling at Athens, is a mere assertion; they may have preceded this passage.

heard of peoples who lived south of the Sahara, but not far enough away to be in the southern temperate zone. But his explanations of why the equator should be cool—the nights are longer than those of summer in more northerly regions, and the sun 'travels faster', i.e. passes over a greater distance of the earth's surface in any given time there than elsewhere—were not plausible. Better was another suggestion, that winds and rains cooled the atmosphere of the equatorial regions.

In reckoning the earth's circumference at 240,000 stades his calculation was based on two incorrect figures, an estimate that the difference of height of the star Canopus seen from Rhodes and from Alexandria is $\frac{1}{48}$ of the zodiac circle, and another that the distance between the two places is 5,000 stades. The two errors work in opposite directions, and if by stade he meant the standard stade of 185 metres, his result is not far out. But the method is unscientific in that he started from figures on which he had no reason to rely; and indeed he probably added that 5,000 stades might be incorrect. By chance the result is better than any other ancient estimate.[1]

He correctly saw that the sun was much larger than the earth and suggested a method for estimating its size, necessarily ineffective because he had no means of determining its distance, for which he had to make an arbitrary assumption. In this great sun, which was pure fire, he saw the cause of much on earth; it created jewels and plants and animals and different races of men, whose characters were associated with their physiques, according to the angle at which its rays fell; for fire has in it a 'vital force'. The earth too contains fire and therefore life. He was greatly interested in volcanoes, the most spectacular evi-

[1]The procedure is inferior to that of Eratosthenes, who had worked more than a century earlier, being based on premises that involve a greater margin of error; hence some modern writers suppose that his object was not to give a more accurate figure. Elsewhere he is reported as saying that the minimum size of the earth's circumference was 180,000 stades. This figure could be obtained by combining the fraction $\frac{1}{48}$ with Eratosthenes' distance between Rhodes and Alexandria, namely 3,750 stades. If it *was* so reached, it looks like a blunder. Eratosthenes' figure was deduced from his own estimate of the earth's circumference as 252,000 stades, combined with the more nearly correct fraction $\frac{1}{60}$.

dence, and noted how well vines grew in their lava. The rhythmical movement of the waves of the sea, which cast out alien bodies, is another sign of life.

But history and geography, like meteorology and geometry, interests which must here be passed over, are subjects that while employing philosophical principles are not the heart of philosophy. That for any Stoic is ethics. In this Posidonius took a new line. He could see no better starting-point than the passions, a familiar reality and urgent practical problem. Justifiably critical of the orthodox Stoic psychology, he reverted to Plato's view that the *psyche* had both rational and irrational elements. The attempt to maintain the unity of the command-centre by interpreting the passions as false judgments or their results was incompatible with the facts of experience and did not allow any plausible explanation of how passions arose or were overcome. Once again Posidonius wanted to penetrate to causes. He pointed out that the same false judgment may be accompanied by passion one day, but not on another. Why do passions die down, although the judgment persists? In animals and children we can see the domination of irrational forces; is it likely that these should disappear with the coming of reason? On the contrary they remain, and it is they that get out of hand and cause the impulses that are 'disobedient to reason'. We have inborn desires for pleasure and for power, which give rise to the passions, 'excessive impulses', which need to be restrained by reason. These are not parts, but capacities of the *psyche,* which is a single substance capable of various activities. A false judgment may be associated with a passion, but as its result rather than its cause; the 'emotional pull' carries reason off its right course. Now the desires of the irrational elements can be satisfied, pleasures obtained or victory achieved. The passion will then die down, although the judgment, say that a certain pleasure is good, will remain. Another cause for the ceasing of passion is weariness. A runaway horse grows tired of galloping, and similarly a runaway passion will in time lose its force. To recognise these irrational capacities also allows us to explain how men can be bad and passionate. If reason is the sole factor its perversion is not intelligible. Realistically Posidonius called attention to the facts of human development. The child has a natural affinity for pleasure and aversion from pain and a desire for power;

when small it is a creature of passion, kicking and biting to get its own way. As it grows older, it begins to have feelings of shame and to want to be good; it discovers a new affinity, but without losing the former ones. It is in them that the source of evil is to be found.

To the orthodox Stoic, passion, as the result of a faulty judgment, was to be cured or prevented by an appeal to the intellect; fear of death for example, could be stopped by proving to the sufferer that death was not a bad thing. Posidonius, seeing the root of passions in irrational capacities of the *psyche,* did not suppose that they could be reasoned away. The irrational must be treated otherwise. Detailed information about his therapeutic methods is scant. But they seem to have involved treatment both of the passion itself, which could be compared to a passing illness, and of the irrational capacity, much as one might strengthen a man's constitution to enable him to resist disease.[1] He probably thought that diet could affect the irrational elements of the *psyche,* and he praised Plato's methods of training it by physical exercise and by music.

The recognition of irrational forces in the human *psyche,* shared with brute animals, was one factor that led Posidonius to his conception of how men should live. The other was his conviction that human reason is of a different order from such reasoning as is seen in other animals. It is akin to the reason that rules the whole world. Misery, then, lies in not following throughout this god[2] within us, but being sometimes carried

[1] The comparison of passion to physical disease was an old one. But whereas Chrysippus had compared the state of an ordinary imperfect man to that of an unhealthy man, liable to fall ill, Posidonius thought him like a physically normal man; the one may suffer a passing attack of passion, as the other a passing attack of fever. An impaired physical constitution makes a man liable to a particular disease, and an impaired moral constitution to a particular passion. Any man may be angry, but irascible men are easily and frequently angry.

[2] Posidonius' word was *daimon,* a word originally synonymous with *theos* (God), but long used of a being intermediary between gods and men. But since Posidonius emphasised the likeness of the *daimon* to the divine ruler of the world, the rendering 'god' will not be misleading.

away off course with the worse and irrational element. The end for man is 'to live in contemplation of the truth and order of the universe, co-operating so far as possible in bringing it about, and in no way led by the irrational in the *psyche*'. This he regarded as a correct interpretation of the old formula of 'living consistently'. His innovations were to place more emphasis on active co-operation with the world-order, as opposed to mere falling in with it, and explicitly to require the complete subordination of the irrational. Subordination, not extinction; it had a part to play, to which it was to be trained by habituation.

Many Greeks believed that in the history of human society morality had decayed, and Posidonius was one of them. In the world of nature, he said, the leader of the herd is its best member: among animals the most vigorous or the largest, among men the most intelligent. There had been a primitive golden age when wise men ruled, providently, bravely, and beneficially. But vices crept in; kings became tyrants, and the need arose for law; yet the first law-givers were still wise men or philosophers. These early wise men had also discovered the basic arts of civilisation: to build houses, to make nets and train dogs for hunting, to turn ores into iron and bronze, to invent weaving and baking. Seneca, who reports this (*Letter* 90), could not accept it: for him such occupations were below the dignity of a wise man; technical inventions were the road to extravagant luxury; the recent invention of glass-blowing had not been made by philosophers. He agreed that there had been a golden age, but then all men shared in concord the fruits of the earth, living without fear among the beauties of nature, sleeping softly on the hard ground beneath the stars. They were innocent men, but not wise men; for virtue requires a trained, informed, and exercised mind. This fanciful picture of happy primitive man would have had no appeal for Posidonius. He recognised that material civilisation was valuable; from that it followed that the wise man would promote it. His unflagging curiosity interested him in technical processes, which he described in detail. The wise man will apply his mind in all fields. Posidonius would have subscribed to the saying 'knowledge is indivisible'.

To estimate Posidonius' importance, whether absolutely or for the later world, is difficult, because his teaching is very unevenly represented in our sources and there is no agreement about the extent of his influence. His range of vision, his interest in facts, his desire to build a system in which the parts mutually supported one another, remind one of Aristotle. But, unlike Aristotle, he was not profoundly original. His leading ideas, like 'cosmic sympathy' and the partition of the psychic faculties, were taken from others, although applied with thoroughness and independence. There is a recently fashionable tendency to build upon the judgment of Galen, who called him 'the most scientific of the Stoics' and noted that he had been trained in geometry and was accustomed to give demonstrative proofs (*Views of Hippocrates and Plato*, iv 390). But before we hasten to make a great scientist of him, it should be remembered that he has several times appeared as careless of basic facts. There is no doubt that he understood the value of gathering evidence; it is less certain that he realised the importance of gathering all that was feasible and of testing the reliability of hearsay information. His wide range may explain this weakness, but as a scientist he was an amateur compared with an Eratosthenes. Still less right is it to see in him a mystic, a falsity now fortunately obsolescent.[1] What can be put to his credit is a readiness to adapt the Stoic doctrine where it seemed to him indefensible, openly and with a search for the truth not for the minimum change necessary to evade the immediate attack, and a desire to understand in detail this physical world which he believed to be the work of divine reason and therefore intelligible to the kindred human mind.

What influence did this have? So far as the Stoics were concerned, not very much. Doxographers added his name when he had maintained the original doctrine and in addition quote his authority on astronomy, meteorology, seismology. But his recognition of irrational factors in the *psyche* was simply disregarded, and inquiry into the world of nature had little attraction for most of his successors. Seneca's *Problems of Nature* provides

[1]A strange sentence, on which much has been built, although it is no more than a guess that it derives from him, must be mentioned: 'at any rate, leaving their tabernacles of the sun, they (sc. the souls) inhabit the region beneath the moon' (Sextus, *Against the Dogmatists* 9.71). The context is one of life after death and the tabernacles must be earthly tabernacles. I agree with those who think the sun out of place here and its presence in the text due to some mistake.

an exception, but even this work contains little personal observation; it takes the opinions of predecessors and discusses them on their intrinsic merits; moreover each book has a climax in a rhetorical piece of irrelevant moralising. Posidonius may have helped to popularise the idea of the god within man, but otherwise there is no trace of him in Epictetus or Marcus Aurelius. Outside the Stoic school his scientific work was used, often no doubt indirectly; and it has been guessed that he influenced the climate of opinion to take an interest in the wonders of nature. But that his philosophic thought had any effect on the development of Platonism or on Plotinus or on fathers of the Church remains unproven.

9

Stoics and Politics

THAT philosophy could teach statesmanship was Plato's firm belief. He himself unsuccessfully attempted to guide Dionysius II at Syracuse, and members of the Academy gave advice at several less prominent places. There were monarchs who felt that philosophers had something to offer; at the lowest their presence would add lustre to the court. Philip of Macedon's motives in obtaining Aristotle as an instructor of the boy Alexander at Pella must remain as obscure as those of Alexander himself in taking Aristotle's pupil Callisthenes to Persia. When Antigonus Gonatas asked Zeno to come to Macedon, his invitation was based on real admiration; he may have hoped not only for his company but also that he would exercise a good influence on the men at court. Zeno would not go, but sent Philonides and his young pupil Persaeus, whom Antigonus in course of time made civil governor of Corinth, one of the Macedonian garrison-towns. When Corinth was captured by Aratus of Sicyon in 243 BC, he either died fighting, as some later Stoics believed, or got away in the confusion, as more hostile sources claimed. He was not the military commander, as was maliciously alleged later, and nothing is known of his administration. But he wrote a book on kingship, another about the Spartan constitution, and a long attack on Plato's *Laws*. Soon after the fall of Corinth another of Zeno's pupils, Sphaerus, already an old man, went to Sparta, where he tried to influence the young; he was admired by Cleomenes, who came to the throne in 235, and became associated with him in his reforms. He is also said to have been invited to the court of Ptolemy IV Philopator in Egypt, but the truth may be that he took refuge there with Cleomenes when the latter had to leave Sparta in 221. It is possible, however, that he went earlier, at the request of Ptolemy III Euergetes, since the invitation is said to have come while Cleanthes was still alive. Chrysippus, so it is reported, then refused to go; but the refusal was not based on principle, since he regarded service with a king as a suitable source of income for a wise man.

Although these minor figures had parts in the political scene, it was remarked that neither Zeno nor Cleanthes nor Chrysippus, who all declared that a man should take part in the political life of his city, ever did anything of the kind at Athens. They were of course foreigners, but it was believed that the first two could have had citizenship if they had wanted it, and Chrysippus in fact acquired it. Perhaps they felt that there was not much they could achieve in a democracy, even in the limited democracy which was all that Athens enjoyed in much of the third century. An anecdote represents Chrysippus as answering, when asked why he took no part in political life, that bad politics would displease the gods and good politics the citizens. To act by influencing a sympathetic autocrat or powerful man might seem to offer a more effective means of doing good. Nevertheless Chrysippus said that a wise man would take part in political life, unless there was some obstacle, and that he would there speak and act as if wealth, health, and reputation were all good things. In other words, to be effective, he must use the language of his hearers.

It is not to be supposed that there was any Stoic political programme. Politics are largely concerned with obtaining or providing power, status, or material things the value of which the Stoics recognised, it is true, but depreciated. The real interest of these philosophic advisers was with men's moral welfare, and it may be imagined that their energies were mainly devoted not to current issues but to more general preaching against fear, anger, and cupidity, in favour of self-control and philanthropy. A figure who may form a partial exception is Blossius, an Italian from Cumae and pupil of Antipater of Tarsus; it was widely said that along with one Diophanes, a rhetorician from Mytilene, he urged Tiberius Gracchus on to his land reforms. After Tiberius' death he joined Aristonicus, who was trying to maintain the independence of Pergamum, left to the Romans by its last king Attalus III; on the failure of this enterprise he committed suicide. It may be guessed that Blossius was politically committed, both in Rome and in Pergamum, although the only piece of advice specifically ascribed to him was a protest to Tiberius on the day of his assassination, urging him not to be intimidated by a crow that had ominously dropped a stone in front of him.

Blossius was not the first philosopher to be associated with a Roman politician. When in the later second century BC many Romans began to take an interest in Greek culture, some leading men became the patrons of Greeks whose profession was philosophy. Panaetius had by 140 BC established a firm friendship with the younger Scipio, who in that year took him as his sole companion on a mission to Alexandria and the East; through Scipio he exerted an influence on several eminent Romans, who accepted Stoicism as a guide. In the next century Cicero, although he professed to be a sceptic, took a Stoic philosopher Diodotus into his house and maintained him until he died. Even Pompey thought it proper when in the East to go and hear Posidonius at Rhodes. But the younger Cato, a declared Stoic, was the patron of at least three philosophers of that school, Antipater of Tyre, Apollonides, who was with him at his death, and Athenodorus of Tarsus, nicknamed 'Knobby', whom he induced to leave the post of librarian at Pergamum and accompany him to Rome.

Cato was a member of an old family and its traditions destined him for a political life. He attempted to conduct himself according to Stoic principles and what he regarded as old Roman standards. He lived simply and even when praetor sometimes went barefoot and without a tunic. In the anarchy of the later years of the Republic he held firm again and again to the view that the law must be respected, showing great courage in the physical dangers to which this exposed him. Admired for his financial honesty, he made enemies by his attempts to impose it on others. No doubt he was mistaken in thinking it practicable to restore respect for the law and an out-of-date constitution; too much power belonged to those whose interests lay in disregarding them.[1] He was elected to a series of offices but failed to win the consulship. To the usual bargaining, compromising politician he would seem an obstinate doctrinaire. Yet in the final resort, if it was impossible to preserve legality, he

[1] A modern historian may also observe that the law gave unjustifiable privileges to the small ruling class to which he belonged. But that does not make him a hypocrite.

would give in: he opposed the claims both of Caesar and of Pompey, but in the end, seeing the greater danger in Caesar and in Pompey the only means of stopping him, he accepted the latter as sole consul, unconstitutional as this was, ready to support him loyally for the time.

After Pompey's death he took some troops by a famous march across the Libyan desert to join those who were resisting Caesar in North Africa, where he handed over the command to a young Scipio who as an ex-consul outranked him. On Scipio's defeat at Thapsus Cato, who had remained at Utica, sent his senatorial friends back to Italy to make their peace but decided that he must take his own life since he could no longer live in the way appropriate for him. After reading Plato's *Phaedo*, he stabbed himself with a sword recovered with great difficulty from friends who wished to frustrate his intention. When he lost consciousness they tried to bind him up, but on coming to he tore his wounds open with his bare hands and so perished. His career and above all his death made him a hero: he had shown himself to be unconquerable by adversity. For later Roman Stoics of the upper classes he became the ideal prototype, the man who lived and died as reason and conscience dictated.

Another Athenodorus, also from Tarsus, known as 'the Bald', had a career worth recounting as it shows what a professional philosopher might at this time achieve. Probably a pupil of Posidonius, he was appealed to by Cicero for help with the third book of his work *On Duties*; having taught the young Octavian, the future Augustus, he became his adviser after his elevation to be head of the state; there are stories that he told him to govern his temper by saying over the letters of the alphabet before making a decision, and that he once substituted himself for a senator's wife with whom the emperor had an assignation, emerging to the other's consternation from her closed litter. In his later years he returned to Tarsus with a commission to change its constitution—the town was under demagogic control; he obtained for it relief from taxation and when he died was given a hero's cult there. Another Stoic, Arius Didymus, was maintained by Augustus and befriended by Maecenas; we have extracts from his summaries of Stoic and of Peripatetic doctrines; Seneca reports that the emperor's wife Livia had more comfort from him at the death of her son Drusus than from any other source (*Consolation to Marcia* 4).

Some wealthy Romans, it is clear, found it useful to keep a philosopher, and men of distinction did not find the position humiliating. They expected to be able to give moral advice and comfort to their patrons and their families, while their patrons could draw strength from their approval. The relation between Seneca and Nero had some similar elements, although Seneca was not only a philosopher but also a Roman, ambitious and anxious to play his own part in political life. When he found his position too difficult and attempted to retire, Nero would not let him go, stressing, if Tacitus can be believed, the value of the philosopher's counsel and the danger to his own reputation should Seneca leave him (*Annals* 14, 55–6).

Many Romans were, however, deeply suspicious of philosophy and philosophers. Both Nero and Agricola were warned against the subject by their mothers, and other instances of criticism and prejudice would make a long catalogue. Important though the relation between some leading men and philosophers was, hostility was at least as powerful a force. No sooner had Seneca fallen from favour than an attack was made on Rubellius Plautus, like Nero a grandson of Augustus' stepson. He was living quietly in Asia, but was said to have 'assumed the arrogance of the Stoics, a sect that turns men into mutinous trouble-makers'. He refused to try to raise a revolt, but followed the course recommended by his attendant philosophers, Coeranus and Musonius (see p. 162), who advised him to meet death bravely, not to prolong life's alarms and uncertainties. He was murdered by a centurion sent to kill him. His friend Barea Soranus, another Stoic, who had been a just governor of Asia Minor, was accused of treasonable intentions in winning the favour of the provincials, and allowed to commit suicide. The same fate befell Thrasea Paetus, a Stoic who had walked out of the senate when motions were proposed for celebrating the murder of Agrippina. For three years he did not attend its meetings, and he gathered round himself followers who imitated his austere dress and solemn face: this was represented as a challenge to the Emperor's way of life. These self-declared champions of liberty, it was said, would overthrow the Empire, and when it was overthrown, attack the liberty of others.

It would be a mistake to treat these last accusations too seriously and to suppose that Thrasea and his friends had any thought of overthrowing the Empire or establishing a Stoic tyranny, or indeed that there was any Stoic political programme. The liberty that they claimed was not one which they lacked or of which they could be deprived: it was the liberty to act according to conscience, not freedom from the consequences of so acting. Thrasea found himself unable to join in the flatteries heaped on Nero by his fellow senators or to defend the crimes that they approved at the Emperor's orders: he was therefore an opponent, although a passive one, of this princeps;[1] but that did not make him an opponent of the principate. If he had had the fortune to live under the rule of Hadrian or even of Vespasian, he might have had a useful career and been forgotten by history.

A more radical character was Helvidius Priscus, Thrasea's son-in-law, who as a young man attached himself to the Stoics, in order to carry himself firmly among the dangers of political life. He was determined always to champion what he saw as right, which included the independence of the Senate. Once he there opposed the emperor Vitellius, who attended even its less important meetings; at the accession of Vespasian his honorific speech kept within the bounds of truth; shortly afterwards, when the Capitol needed restoration, he proposed that the emperor should susidise the empty public purse but that the Senate should retain control of the work. When an opportunity offered, he attacked Marcellus Eprius, who had played a part in Thrasea's fall. He had the approval of the Senate, which was eager to punish those of its members who had profited by Nero's reign of terror, unlike Vespasian, who wished old enmities to be forgotten; Marcellus left the meeting, saying: 'I leave your Senate to you, Priscus; act the king there, in Caesar's presence.'[2]

Helvidius was a praetor, whereas Vespasian held no magistracy; accordingly he openly criticised the emperor, treating

---

[1]*Princeps* means 'leading man' in the state. It was a smooth word which disguised the fact that Rome had a ruler whose power became increasingly absolute.

[2]The emperors took the name of Caesar.

him as if he had been an ordinary senator. He is said to have denounced monarchy and praised democracy. Rome had never known anything that we or the Greeks would have called democracy, and one may guess that if Helvidius used the word he thought that the Senate would adequately express the will of the people. The Emperor's authority was *de facto* rather than *de jure*; Helvidius seems to have had the impracticable idea that constitutional theory should prevail over the facts of power. There is no suggestion in the ancient sources that he was the leader of a party of any importance. But he was dangerous because he was a bad example; the Emperor required a subservient Senate, not an opposition.[1]

Before long Helvidius was banished and then put to death, perhaps on the order of the Senate itself. More than that all teachers of philosophy, except Musonius, were excluded from Rome; the Stoics were denounced as self-important men who thought that a beard and rough cloak and bare feet made them wise, brave, and just, who looked down on their fellow-men, calling the well-born spoilt children, and the base-born men of no spirit, the beautiful indecent and the ugly gifted, the rich greedy and the poor slavish. This picture, or caricature, has some of its colour from acquaintance with Cynics, one of whom, Demetrius, was prominent at Rome at this time. They had affinities with the Stoics (see pp. 20, 170) but were anarchists on principle, who believed that the price of happiness was to shake off man-made law and convention. In AD 75 two Cynics got back into the city: one rose in the theatre to denounce the spectators and was whipped; the second was beheaded. Under Domitian Junius Rusticus, a senator, was executed because he had praised Thrasea and Helvidius: this was made the occasion to banish all philosophers from the whole of Italy.

[1]Epictetus shows no interest in Helvidius' political ideas, only in his personal autonomy. His story is that Vespasian told him not to attend a meeting of the Senate: 'So long as I am a senator, I must come.' 'Come, but keep quiet.' 'Don't ask me my views and I will say nothing.' 'But I am bound to ask you.' 'And I to say what I think right.' 'Then I shall put you to death.' 'Did I ever tell you I was immortal? You will do your part, and I shall do mine' (*Discourses* I.2.19–21).

STOICS AND POLITICS

In the century of enlightened government that followed after Domitian's tyranny philosophers regained their old place, and were widely, although not universally, accepted as educators and advisers, and valued as guides to conduct. The emperor Hadrian probably founded professorships for philosophy,[1] and certainly provided the young Marcus Aurelius with his first philosophic teachers. Antoninus Pius, too, brought the eminent Stoic Apollonius to Rome as the young man's instructor. There the philosopher insisted that the young prince should wait on him, not be visited in the palace. Marcus mentions among other mentors Q. Junius Rusticus, no doubt related to the man of the same name executed by Domitian, a prominent figure in public life and later to be Prefect of the City, who introduced him to Epictetus' *Discourses,* lending his own copy, and Sextus, Plutarch's nephew, but a Stoic in spite of his uncle's determined opposition to the school.

If it is asked what effect these teachers, of whom most were Stoics, had upon politics and social conditions, one cannot point to any specific piece of legislature or social change. Stoic ethics were primarily concerned with the individual, and the object of moral teaching was to make him a better man. More and more this came to be looked on as a matter of ridding him of his passions; they were psychological diseases and the philosopher was the doctor of the soul. Stoics might hold that some men, whose social position called them to it, had the duty of playing a role in political life. When the younger Pliny complained to the respected Stoic teacher Euphrates of the burden of public duties, he was told that they were the finest part of philosophy (*Letters* 1.10). But Stoicism had no sort of political programme; there was only the generalised injunction to act sensibly and justly. Nor was a Stoic likely to be filled with a desire to improve men's material conditions; his principles told him that they were irrelevant to their welfare, common opinion regarded them as incapable of much improvement, and his philosophy took them to be the work of Providence.

[1]Significantly he was the first Roman emperor to wear a beard, a practice continued by his successors down to and including Septimius Severus.

Nevertheless Stoicism must have had some undefinable general influence that favoured conscientious administration for the benefit of the ordinary man and a humanitarianism that resulted in a little legislation and some charitable foundations. The Greco–Roman world would have been a worse place without its philosophers.

10

The Later Stoics

The first two centuries AD were the age which produced the greater part of the Stoic literature that still survives. Its authors were very varied. Some made their teaching or writing their main business; these included Musonius, a well-to-do man from Etruria, Epictetus, a Greek freedman, and probably Hierocles, of whose life nothing is known. Seneca was a spare-time amateur philosopher and Marcus Aurelius was the Emperor. But, with the possible exception of Hierocles, they had in common a close connexion with Rome, where they were all introduced to philosophy. The capital city was a place where teachers of Stoicism were active; little is known of them beyond the names of a number. Yet it may be supposed that like their pupils they saw in Stoic philosophy an established system of beliefs that would comfort, guide, and support a man in the difficulties and dangers of life.

SENECA

No Stoic author has exerted a greater influence on posterity than Seneca. Because he wrote in Latin he was immediately accessible to literary men after the revival of learning; his moralising was to the taste of that age; and his epigrammatic, exaggerated style made quotation from him easy and effective. Yet his work as a philosopher, or rather as a writer on themes drawn from philosophy, occupied only a part of his attention; his main interest was in public life; when that was closed to him he turned to writing, persuading himself that this was the better course. It would be wrong to suppose that his thought, speech, and actions as a political figure were unaffected by the philosophical principles that he had learned as a young man; on the other hand his writings cannot be understood without reference to the events of his life.

Born in the year AD 1 at Corduba in Spain, a town with many Roman inhabitants, he was the son of a Seneca whom we distinguish as 'the elder', himself a Roman citizen and an author

with a great interest in the rhetoricians whose ingenious show-
pieces of declamation attracted public attention now that
neither law-courts nor politics offered the same scope to the
orator that they had done under the republic. His father brought
him to Rome as a boy, to study rhetoric and philosophy. He
was deeply moved by his teachers, in particular by Sotio, who
seems to have combined some Pythagorean doctrine with current moralising, by Attalus, a Stoic, and by Papirius Fabianus,
whose copious philosophical writings were adorned by the
stylistic devices of the rhetoric that had once been his sole
pursuit. For a whole year the young Seneca adopted a vegetarian diet on grounds of principle, until his father warned him
that such eccentricity was no recommendation in an aspirant
to a political career. To this he now turned, and filled some
minor offices, but his progress was interrupted by an illness of
which the symptoms were emaciation and acute depression and
which caused him to retire for some years to Egypt. Returning
at the age of thirty, he obtained the quaestorship, entered the
Senate, and by his eloquence there and in the law-courts made
both reputation and money. The accession of the mad Caligula
to the throne in AD 37 made it dangerous to be prominent, and
after conducting a brilliant prosecution he is said to have been
saved from death only by the intervention of one of the emperor's mistresses, who represented the orator as already having
one foot in the grave; his health must again have been impaired. It was not Caligula, but his successor Claudius who
struck a shattering blow. In AD 41 Seneca was accused of
adultery with the emperor's sister, condemned unheard, and
exiled to Corsica. Possibly he was the innocent victim of a
plot by Messalina, Claudius' wife, and the powerful imperial
freedmen who worked with her. He attempted to console himself with his philosophical principles; he wrote to his mother
Helvia a *Consolation* full of the proper sentiments according
to which exile was no evil but an opportunity, and he tried to
occupy himself with geographical observations and the com-
position of poetry. But he was miserable in his isolation and
when the son of Polybius, one of Claudius' freedmen, died, he
addressed to the father a *Consolation* which was the excuse
for flattering the recipient and the emperor and for pleas for
his own pardon. That, however, had to wait until Messalina

had been replaced by Agrippina, who had him recalled after eight years of exile and put him in charge of the education of her son, the young Nero. She had no liking for philosophy and presumably saw in Seneca a man of letters with experience of public life. In AD 54 Claudius died; Seneca wrote a laudatory memorial speech for Nero to deliver, and took revenge for his exile by the *Apocolocyntosis (pumpkinification)*, a satire on the deification of the dead man, which in the worst of taste makes game of physical disabilities and sneers at his intellectual and moral deficiencies. Seneca had now reached the peak of his career; he had already been a praetor under Claudius and in 56 he was to hold the consulship. But that was more an honour than a position of power; power came from the fact that Nero left a large share of government to him and his friend Burrus, commander of the praetorian guard. They were doubtless right in thinking themselves more competent than the young man, whom they diverted by encouraging his artistic ambitions and a liaison with a freedwoman. Of this Agrippina disapproved; she became estranged and was suspected of plotting to replace Nero by Claudius' son Germanicus, a danger ended by his death, perhaps due to poison. But Nero became increasingly independent and his actions increasingly criminal; in 59, having failed in an attempt to have his mother 'accidentally' drowned, he feared that she might strike back by attempting a revolution. Seneca, according to Tacitus, asked Burrus whether the troops could be commanded to kill her; he replied that they had too much sympathy for her, and her death was entrusted to a freedman officer of the fleet and reported to the Senate by the emperor in a message clearly written by the philosopher.

The death of Burrus in 62 left Seneca, already the object of attack by envious senators, in an exposed position and he asked to be allowed to retire and to return the wealth he had acquired from the emperor. The request was refused, but effectively he withdrew from public affairs to busy himself with what are perhaps the most substantial of his writings, *Questions about Nature* and *Letters on Morality*, both addressed to his younger friend Lucilius. Accused in 65 of complicity in the conspiracy of Piso, he felt that he had no option but to obey Nero's command to commit suicide.

Thus although ideas drawn from philosophers were always of importance to Seneca, primarily he was not a philosopher but a rhetorician, a senator, a man at the heart of public affairs. His writings often sprang from his own situations to meet his own needs. Unfortunately many cannot be securely dated, but of some the occasion is clear.

On Anger (*c.* AD 41) is a show-piece, addressed to his elder brother, who was the Gallio before whom St Paul was arraigned in Corinth. In the first book anger is defined and denounced; the Peripatetic view that in moderation it is a useful emotion is attacked. The second book begins by examining how anger arises; an apparent injury causes an automatic disturbance of the mind; if that is followed by a judgment that an injury has been suffered and ought to be punished, the disturbance becomes a drive that gets out of hand and no longer obeys reason. The necessary part played by the judgment gives the assurance that anger can be resisted, for the judgment, which is false, need not be made. If anger were an independent emotion there would be no way of preventing it. The next section returns to the point that anger is neither useful nor defensible; finally advice is given on how to avoid it. The third book opens with the intention of explaining how to check anger in others, but does not reach this subject until the final chapters, being mainly concerned with the restraint of one's own temper. The construction of the whole work is therefore very loose, and Seneca's grasp of his principles is weak: he distinguishes anger from cruelty, but many of his anecdotes illustrate the latter rather than the former; at one point he argues that animals cannot be angry, but at another that there is no beast so dreadful that anger does not make it appear even more savage (I. 1.6, 3.5–7).

On Clemency, apparently written in AD 56[1] (I. 9.1) but never

[1]The passage that dates the work gives false information about the young Octavian. By an ingenious emendation F. Préchac (Budé edn. p. cxxvi) avoids the error and changes the date to AD 55. He believes the work to have been written very shortly after Nero's accession, when he could still be honestly praised. To me this seems to be excluded by too many passages that imply at least some months of power. But as so often with Seneca one cannot be quite confident what is meant.

finished, is addressed to the young Nero and attempts to recommend this traditional Roman virtue. Clemency, says Seneca, is not to be confused with pardon, the remission of a properly determined punishment; it must be wrong to alter a sentence that was correct. Nor is it to be confused with the distracting emotion of pity. 'I know,' he says, 'that the Stoics have a bad reputation among the ignorant as being too hard and most unlikely to give rulers good advice . . . but no school is more kindly, more loving of mankind, more attentive to the common good.' Clemency is to be seen as a rational avoidance of cruelty. Although the regular courts and occasionally the Senate dealt with criminal charges, many cases were left to the emperor's decision. Seneca argues that the right punishment will often be a mild one or none at all: extreme rigour is rarely called for; this after all is the way in which a father brings up his children. Harsh treatment actually encourages crime and exposes the ruler to danger; many criminals will reform if given a chance. He recognises that the emperor can as a matter of fact break the law, and suggests that to break it can be justified; the emperor is the directing mind of the body politic and therefore not to be trammelled by rules. But the important thing is that he should disregard rules only at the dictate of reason, not at that of anger.

The warnings against anger and its offspring cruelty are emphatic enough to make one think that Seneca was not blind to his pupil's weakness. The young prince is frequently praised as an exemplar of clemency and is made to boast that he has spared the blood of even the most worthless men. He is congratulated on his innocence, and told that no individual has ever been so dear to another as he is to the Roman people. Clearly the object of the work is to appeal to his better feelings and to engage him in the path of virtue. But was not the appeal too late? He had already caused the murder of his brother Britannicus early in 55 and begun the nocturnal brawling in the streets that led to the death of Silanus, who had recognised him. Seneca stands accused of flattery and falsehood and must be found guilty. But probably he believed that these subterfuges offered the best hope of drawing Nero back from the dangerous course on which he had entered. Publicly to reprove him could do no good, but he might attempt to preserve an attractive image that was painted for him. Perhaps Seneca abandoned the treatise on realising that this hope was not to be fulfilled.

Three short works are addressed to Serenus, a friend whom he converted from Epicureanism. *The Constancy of the Wise Man* argues that nothing is an injury unless the person attacked thinks it is one; the wise man has neither hopes nor fears; his stability cannot be shaken by external events:

> 'Fortune', says Epicurus, 'rarely touches the wise.' How near he came to saying what a real man would say! Are *you* ready to speak more courageously and put fortune away absolutely? The wise man's cottage, where there is no splendour, no bustle, no elaboration, is guarded by no doorkeepers to sort out the crowd with an insolence that asks to be bribed, but Fortune does not cross that empty threshold on which no janitor stands: she knows there is no place for her where she owns nothing.

This, Seneca continues is no impossible ideal; it was attained, perhaps even exceeded (a typical meaningless exaggeration) by Cato.

Calm of Mind is written with more verve than order. One of the most interesting sections is that in which Seneca reports the opinion of the Stoic Athenodorus, who although favouring political activity in principle thought that in the world as it was the good man had no hope of success; he would be more effective by remaining in private life and preaching virtue. This, Seneca replies, is too pessimistic; if one is forced to retreat from public life, one should do it step by step, understand the limits of one's power and look for a way of being useful within them. This work may have been written during the first years of Nero's reign, and the earlier *Constancy of the Wise* before Seneca's recall from exile, to picture the man he would have liked to be and wished to be thought. These are uncertain guesses; but there can be no doubt that the third work, *On Leisure,* dates from his last years. Only a fragment survives, in which he answers the criticism of Serenus, who reproves him for taking no part in public life. Retirement and quiet have now become the wise man's choice. The intellectual life is preferable to that of action. A lifetime is not enough for the study of nature. Zeno and Chrysippus did more for posterity than if they had commanded armies or carried laws; they legislated for humanity not for a single state. In the lost conclusion he seems to have maintained that by his public service he had earned his retirement.

The Shortness of Life also recommends turning one's back on business of all kinds. Life is long if one knows how to use it, Paulinus, to whom the work is addressed, is advised to abandon the administration of the corn-supply and retire to quieter, safer, and greater pursuits, the investigation of the laws of nature and the love of virtue. The work apparently belongs to 49; written in Rome, it therefore suggests that Seneca's appointment as Nero's tutor did not immediately follow his recall. *The Happy Life* begins by making happiness the result of virtue and then develops at length the view that pleasure should never be our goal, even a subsidiary goal. From this Seneca turns to an impassioned attack on those who criticise philosophers for not living up to their precepts. Philosophers do not claim to be perfect, but they are immensely superior to their critics. (Seneca adds somewhat unconvincingly that he is not speaking for himself; *he* is sunk in the depth of every vice.) 'If those who follow virtue are avaricious, lustful, ambitious, what are you who hate the very name of virtue?' 'You, who hate virtue and the man who cultivates it, are doing nothing new. Sick eyes fear the sun and nocturnal animals shun the brilliance of the day . . . Groan and exercise your tongues by insulting the good! Gape and bite! You will break your teeth much sooner than make any mark.' There follows a long answer to the question how a philosopher can justify his possession of riches. Here can be heard the accents of self-defence. In 58 a man on trial had attacked Seneca as more guilty than himself: 'what philosophical principles had caused him to acquire 300 million sesterces in less than four years of imperial favour?' He replies according to orthodox Stoic teaching that wealth, although not a good, is not to be rejected or despised; it allows virtue a wider field of action. It must of course be honestly acquired and properly used; to give money away correctly is no easy task. What matters above all is the right mental attitude:

Place me in the wealthiest home, where gold and silver are in common use: I shall not think well of myself for that; they may be in my house, but they are not in me. Remove me to the Bridge of Piles and set me among the destitute: I shall not despise myself because I am seated among those who stretch out their hand for alms. If a man does not lack the power to die, what does he care if he lacks a crust? But what follows from this? I still prefer that splendid home to the bridge ... I shall not believe myself a scrap happier because I have a soft pillow and my guests lie on purple; I shall not be a scrap more miserable if my tired shoulders rest on a handful of straw. But what follows from this? I would still rather show what sort of a spirit I have in a magistrate's cloak than with a bare back (25. 1–2).

On Providence seems to be late also; like *Questions about Nature* and *Letters on Morality*, it is addressed to Lucilius, who is represented as asking why many evils befall good men, if Providence rules the world. In his reply Seneca uses the terms 'evil' and 'good' now in the narrow Stoic sense, now in the popular way, which does not make for clarity of expression. But certain ideas stand out. The world of nature is planned and regular, so it would be absurd if Providence did not plan what happens to men. To be virtuous we must not be shaken by those 'inconveniences' that are popularly called 'evils'. Such stability comes only of practice. God therefore exercises those whom he loves, and he welcomes the sight of a great man struggling successfully with calamities. Fortune does not attack the weak, but those who are worthy adversaries. If God were to bring 'evils' upon bad men only, the world would think them truly evil. By giving 'good things' to bad men he shows that they are not truly good. We should not resent anything that happens; it is all predetermined and part of one great plan, in which many 'calamities' are necessary concomitants of what is good. 'There is much that is sad, horrible, hard to bear', complains a recusant. 'Yes', God might reply, 'and since I could not exempt you from such things, I have armed your minds against them all. Bear them bravely. That is how you can surpass God: he cannot suffer evil, you are above suffering it . . . Above all I have seen to it that nothing should detain you against your will.

The way out is open. If you do not wish to fight, you can flee. I have made nothing easier than to die.' (6. 6–7.) The thought that death is a refuge from the stresses and pains of life is characteristic of Seneca; to contemplate death and its inevitability fascinated him; he was glad that we are dying from the moment of our birth. More often than not he believed, or hoped, that the soul would pass on to an abode in the sky; but when it suited his argument, he could declare that death was extinction (e.g. *Letters*, 54. 4–5, 77. 11, 99. 30).

The last of the seven books *On Services Rendered*[1] was written in 64 and the first may be as late as 62. Much attention is paid to the return of help and kindness, to gratitude and ingratitude and their effect on giver and recipient. At times Seneca may have an eye to his relations with Nero, but for the most part he seems to be developing material provided by earlier writers; one of these may be Hecato, who is several times quoted. There is a good deal of casuistry in an attempt to determine what does or does not constitute a service and where the line is to be drawn between gratitude and ingratitude. The work lacks structure; even within a single paragraph Seneca leaps from one thought to another; indeed in search of epigram he sometimes transcends thought. But there is much of interest: illustrative anecdotes drawn from his own lifetime, side-lights on contemporary society, and shrewd psychological observation.

The 124 surviving *Letters on Morality* include some of Seneca's most satisfying writing. The form excuses looseness of construction and excludes excessive elaboration. Particularly in the later letters he tries to state and discuss problems that had exercised Stoic philosophers. In several places here he shows a knowledge of Posidonius, with whom he is not always ready to agree (cf. p. 137). A feature of letters 10–30 is that almost every one contains a quotation from Epicurus. Seneca did not read him to find new ideas, but for the forceful expression of old truths, delighted to find that in spite of false principles he often arrives at correct practical conclusions. These are the property not of his school but of the world.

---

[1] *De Beneficiis*; no English word adequately represents the Latin, which covers gifts, favours, and voluntary services of all kinds.

Written at the same time, namely the last two or three years of Seneca's life, *Questions about Nature* concern themselves with what he regards as the other half of philosophy, for he had no interest in logic. He comes near to claiming that it is the superior half. Knowledge of the physical world, he asserts, is what makes life worth living. One rises above the miseries of the human condition, to know God, who controls everything, as the mind of the universe. But although this escape is possible only for the man who has made moral progress, such a one will not be firm in his contempt for the usual objects of human ambition until his mind has voyaged through the heavens and seen the puny insignificance of the earth. Because he thus recognises the connection of physics and morality, Seneca may have felt himself justified in introducing a number of moral diatribes into this scientific work. But they are arbitrarily attached without any genuine connexion, in one case without even an excuse 'Allow me', he says, 'to put the problem aside and to chastise luxury'. The subjects with which Seneca deals are these: meteors, haloes and rainbows, thunderbolts and thunder, springs and the future flood that will end all life, the Nile, hail and snow, winds, earthquakes, and comets. His treatment of the various topics is deliberately varied; sometimes he simply exposes what he takes to be the truth, at other times he passes in review a large number of previous opinions. He found some material in Posidonius, probably more than he acknowledges; but he did not hesitate also to disagree with him; in general his sources cannot be determined, nor is it clear how much of his argument is his own. So, when he adopts the view that comets are permanent bodies like the planets and that their orbits still await discovery, the considerations he advances against the generally accepted explanation, according to which they are temporary outbreaks of fire, may or may not be original, but in any case he deserves credit for seeing their strength.

Seneca ends his *Questions* by reflecting how little is known or even can be known about the works of God. But 'the people of a coming age will know many things that we do not; much is reserved for the generations to be, when all memory of us has been lost'. Then he turns to moralising: 'the one thing to which we devote our minds completely is not yet achieved, the ultimate in badness; our vices are still on the advance . . . We have not yet quite cast aside our moral fibre; we are still engaged in putting an end to whatever good conduct remains with us.' It is characteristic that not so long before, after a bitter denunciation of the immorality of his times, he had insisted that no age is more than marginally better than another: the amount of crime is almost constant, only its direction changes, as one vice supplants another in popularity (*On Services Rendered* I 9–10). Such inconsistencies are not uncommon: 'he took too little trouble with philosophy', says Quintilian. *On Clemency* makes the emperor boast with Seneca's approval that he has put away *severitas* (sternness) and that when he had found no other reason for showing pity he has spared himself (sc. spared himself the unpleasantness of inflicting punishment); but later in the same work *severitas* is a virtue and pity a vice. Sometimes virtue seems to be within easy reach, at others it is a hardly attainable ideal. Usually he follows Chrysippean orthodoxy in holding that the soul or *psyche* is one and rational, passions being mistaken judgments, but occasionally he distinguishes an independent irrational element.

More than once Seneca declares that he is not bound by orthodoxy. There are however few places where he puts forward views that he claims to be original. Yet there are in his psychology certain features which are first met in him. One perhaps came from Sotio. He recognises that wise man will not be unmoved by external events; just as his body must automatically react to pain, so his soul must react to misfortune; his country's ruin will not leave him untouched and the sight of a loved one lying dead may stir him to weep. But these spontaneous and inevitable feelings are no more than *propatheiai* or preliminaries to passion; passion is an excess which follows on a faulty judgment, and that requires a man's active consent, which the wise man will not give. This analysis took account of the facts of experience and did not demand an impossible and repugnant insensibility;[1] resistance to passion was also made more feasible, since the preliminary feeling gave warning of its possible approach.

Another concept to gain in importance is that of 'will', which

---

[1] Chrysippus may have led the way; see Cicero, *Talks at Tusculum* 3.83, and Aulus Gellius 19.1.14 ff.

Seneca used without considering how it could be fitted into orthodoxy. 'What do you need to be good?' 'The will to be good'. 'A large part of progress is to have the will to advance; I am conscious of that; I will it and will it with all my mind.' 'You cannot be taught to will.' This is something new in Stoicism, which had been marked by an exaggerated intellectualism. A further important concept is that of 'conscience'. By that he means awareness of having done right or wrong; the one is a 'good conscience' and the reward of doing right, more important than reputation or repayment, whereas awareness of wrong-doing brings fear, which is a proof that we have a natural abhorrence of crime. He does not mean by the word any inner monitor or judge, although he believes that there is such an element within man; the mind can examine itself. He recounts how he had learned this habit from Sextius:

> How peaceful, how deep and undisturbed is the sleep that follows on self-examination, when the mind has been given its praise or admonition and, acting as its own secret investigator or censor, has passed judgment on its own character. Every day I put my own case to myself: when the light has been removed and my wife, who knows my habit, has fallen silent, I examine my whole day, go over my doings and my sayings; I hide nothing from myself and I pass nothing over (*On Anger* 3.36).

For posterity Seneca was a dramatist as much as a moralist. His eight, perhaps nine,[1] tragedies were powerful influences in the sixteenth century and then on the French classical drama. Not unexpectedly there are to be found in them ideas that were entertained by philosophers and by Stoics in particular, the dangers of wealth, power, and luxury, the value of a simple life, the blinding effects of passion, the ineluctability of Fate. But that does not make them Stoic dramas. The exception is *Hercules on Oeta*, in which the hero has many of the traits of the Stoic ideal man; but its authenticity is disputed, since in other ways it is unlike the rest. They, although touched by Seneca's knowledge of philosophy, are primarily dramatic. They are concerned

[1] A tenth, *Octavia*, cannot be by him.

with the effects of the passions and the blows of Fortune. For the Stoic Fortune was to be identified with Fate and Providence, for the dramatist it is a blind and hostile power; for the Stoic the passions are sequels of faulty judgment, for the dramatist they are independent forces that fight with reason and pervert it for their own ends. Seneca's characters are not so much human beings as simplified exponents of anger, jealousy, cruelty, fear, pride, and the no less dangerous love, passions which brush aside the arguments of those who speak for reason and moderation. To depict these things he uses all the resources he has learnt from his rhetorical training; short, sharp exchanges, long speeches of self-analysis, epigram, antithesis, exaggeration. He piles on the agony and tries to make his words create an atmosphere of horror, with which the usually quiet intermezzi of the chorus contrast.

Neither the date nor the purpose of these tragedies is known. It is no more than a guess that some at least were written during his exile. That they were not intended for the stage is often asserted and may be true, but does not follow from their nature. One age will welcome plays that another will find intolerable. Certainly Seneca made scenes follow one another arbitrarily, was not concerned to account for his characters' coming and going, relied on verbal, not visual, effects, required as knowledge of mythology in his audience. But, for anything that is known, these may have been characteristics of later Greek tragedy. Many scholars suppose that Senecan tragedy was meant for private declamation. But what will hold the attention if declaimed will be even more gripping if acted. A declamation, however, was easy to arrange; we do not know what were the opportunities for a theatrical performance.

It is hard for the Englishman of today to approach Seneca with sympathy. The distasteful flatteries by which he tried to secure his return from exile and the mockery in *The Pumpkinification* of the late emperor's physical disabilities do not recommend him. As Nero's tutor or mentor he maintained his position by acquiescing in crimes that culminated in matricide, and during the ten years of power or influence accumulated for himself a huge fortune. His sudden and forcible calling-in of loans that he had made to leading Britons was among the causes of Boadicea's revolt.[1] When this man writes books of moralising they hardly ring true. Nor are they helped by his style; as Seneca piles epigram upon epigram, we sense his satisfaction with his own cleverness and remember that he had been trained by rhetoricians as well as the Stoic teachers Sotio and Attalus. He seems insincere and a windbag, 'repeating the same sentiment a thousand times dressed up in different ways' (Fronto p. 157 N).

Yet he deserves pity and understanding. Driven by ambition, struggling with ill-health, surrounded by the temptations and the dangers of a rotten society, he found that philosophic exhortations to virtue too often shed but a feeble light. It is rarely that among the choices open to a man of affairs there is any that is entirely good: frequently he must accept the least of the possible evils. There is no place in politics for perfection. Thrasea Paetus may have kept his conscience clean, but he achieved nothing but his own death. Seneca may have smirched himself more than he need, but he deserves some credit for the Quinquennium Neronis, the period of good administration with which the reign opened. His philosophy was a fitful guide, but he would have been a worse and an unhappier man without it.

MUSONIUS

C. Musonius Rufus took up the teaching of philosophy, a career usually left to Greeks, and his pupils ranged from the slave Epictetus to the future consul C. Minucius Fundanus. But he was not merely a teacher; he tried to take a part in public affairs. Suspected of involvement in the conspiracy of Piso, he was banished by Nero to the barren island of Gyarus. Recalled by Galba, he went out to meet Vespasian's approaching army outside Rome and attempted to preach the blessings of peace to the common soldiers, who treated him with ribaldry. Later in the same year he prosecuted Egnatius Celer, a professed Stoic who had given false evidence against Barea Soranus. Vespasian exempted him from the expulsion of philosophers in 71 AD but later withdrew the exemption. He is not known to have written

---

[1]Dio Cassius 62.2. I keep the traditional name Boadicea for this queen of the Iceni, a tribe of eastern Britain — Boudicca is more correct.

anything; his influence must have been due to his personality. A pupil, one Lucius, used Greek (which may have been the language of Musonius' discourses) to record some of his teaching; extracts survive, all being practical moralising, in which specifically Stoic doctrine has a very narrow place. He makes some use of the denial that anything morally indifferent is good or bad: the proofs of this should, he says, constantly be repeated; it is a truth which demonstrates that exile cannot rob a man of anything really good. But Lucius does not make him insist that only a perfect man can be called good; he says that the philosopher claims to be a good man and he talks as if virtue were in reach.

His practical advice urges simplicity of life: the hair should be cut only enough to avoid discomfort or inconvenience; food should be simple, preferably uncooked, and vegetarian (the exhalations of meat are bad for the intellect); fancy foods are not required even by the sick, since slaves are treated without the use of such diets; clothes should be for protection, not show, to harden not to spoil the body; if you can go without shirt or shoes, so much the better. One would like to know how much effect this had on his hearers' conduct. At the least dislike of extravagance must have been fortified; at the most there were at this time followers of 'philosophy' whose thick beards and unshod feet marked them out from the common run of those with whom they associated.

Musonius' views on marriage throw some light on attitudes of his time. He condemns refusal to let more than the first-born children of a marriage live, less on moral grounds than because a large family is more powerful. He thinks it shameful for a husband to have sexual intercourse with slaves, a thing not allowed to the wife; in fact he regards pleasure as a bad reason for intercourse, which should be for the sake of procreation. Yet he speaks even more warmly than Antipater had done (p. 118) of the joys of marriage. 'What comrade gives his comrade such pleasure as a wife after his heart gives a married man? What brother so pleases his brother, what son his parents? Who longs for an absent one as a man does for his wife and a wife for her husband?'

In a discussion of how a philosopher may best make a living, Musonius recommends employment as a shepherd. There may not in fact have been any Stoic shepherds and Musonius had himself no intention of taking to the hills. But the advice is a reminder that philosophy is seen as an activity that needs neither books nor discussion nor an audience, and that the word 'philosopher' covers both the 'professional' teacher and his pupil, who may want no more than a framework of belief to guide his life, whether that be in politics or withdrawn from the world.

EPICTETUS

Epictetus, a slave from Phrygia, belonged to Nero's freedman Epaphroditus; on being liberated, he became a teacher of Stoicism, to which he had been converted by Musonius. When Domitian banished philosophers from the capital (AD 92 or 95), he withdrew to Nicopolis on the eastern shore of the Adriatic, where many people came to hear him. Among them was the historian and future administrator Arrian, who published eight volumes of his *Discourses*, based on short-hand notes made about 115. Four of those volumes survive, to give a vivid picture of his personality, his methods of teaching, and his pupils. The *Discourses* do not reproduce his formal instruction, which was systematic and based on the classic writings of the early Stoics. They may be called short sermons, some prompted by a question from a pupil, others by the presence of someone who is preached at; but of most the occasion is not recorded. Homely illustrations, imaginary dialogue, vigour and indeed fervour of language, combine to make even the printed word remarkably effective; those who heard him, Arrian reports, could not help but feel exactly what he wanted them to feel. Although these are occasional talks, they are unified by the repetition in constantly varied guise of certain principles which for Epictetus constitute the essence of his message.[1]

[1]There is also *The Handbook*, a selection made by Arrian of 53 extracts, some slightly modified, from the whole work. This became very popular; the neo-Platonist Simplicius' commentary (*c.* AD 535) and two Christianised versions, one doubtfully ascribed to St. Nilus (*c.* AD 430), still survive. In the modern world there have been numerous editions and translations into many languages. Not only was Epictetus a powerful influence on thinkers such as Pascal, but he was also, and more remarkably, admired by men of action, Touissant l'Ouverture and Frederick the Great.

The most important of his beliefs is the distinction between what is in man's power and what is not:

> In our power are our way of thinking, conation, appetition, and aversion; in a word all that is *our* doing. Not in our power are our body, our possessions, reputation and office; in a word all that is not our doing. What is in our power is of its nature free; it cannot be prevented, it cannot be hindered. What is not in our power is weak, the slave of circumstance, liable to be stopped, in the control of others. Remember then that if you take to be free what is of its nature enslaved and think what belongs to others to be your own, you will be obstructed, you will grieve, you will be disturbed, you will blame gods and men; but if you think that nothing is yours but what is yours and that the alien is alien, no one will ever compel you, no one will stop you, you will blame no one, you will do nothing against your will, no one will harm you, you will have no enemy, for you will suffer no hurt (*Handbook* 1).

Freedom is a word ever recurring in Epictetus. From his personal experience he had learned that although the body might be enslaved, a man could be master of his own thought and make his own decisions and judgments. The mind, he says, is free: man can decide what he wants. Various ideas present themselves or are suggested by others, and happiness depends on the way they are treated. The right way is not to think that things in the external world, which includes one's own body, are good or bad, not to want them or to fear them, but to accept them. One cannot control these things; one must take them as they come. 'Do not try to make what happens happen as you wish, but wish for what happens in the way it happens and then the current of your life will flow easily' (*Handbook* 8).

Essentially what man controls, or in a sense what man is, is his *prohairesis*, his moral purpose or basic choice of principle. Epictetus is the first Stoic known to have made this an important technical term. By it he means a general attitude towards life, an assignment of value which determines the way in which we 'treat our presentations'. This phrase was often used by him, and he takes it for granted that it will be understood. It would seem that what he had in mind was something like this: we receive from the outside world presentations, for example 'there is a gold ring', or 'my son is ill'; within us is a power of 'treating' these, by which we may judge that the gold ring is desirable or that our son's illness is a bad thing. These judgments are wrong; one ought to say 'the ring is unimportant' and 'my son's illness does not harm me'. If a man has the right general principles and holds to them, he will judge as he ought to judge. Not only will he be unaffected by desire and regret, unmoved by the pleasures and pains of the outer world, he will also maintain the independence of his thought, never allowing himself to be lured or forced into conduct that his conscience would not approve.

'Then you philosophers inculcate contempt for the governors of the state?' Heaven forbid! Which of us teaches men to dispute the rulers' rights over what is in their power? Take my wretched body, take my property, my reputation, those who are near me. 'Yes, but I want to rule your thoughts too.' And who has given you that power? How can you overcome another man's thought? 'I shall overcome it by intimidation.' You do not know that thought can be overcome by itself, but by nothing else (*Discourses* I. 29. 9–12).

Although he accepted the orthodox view that there were differences in the normal values of external things, Epictetus' sharp distinction between them and man's internal life led to a certain depreciation of those values. He saw moral life more in terms of gladly accepting all that happened to one than in those of trying to acquire the things that accord with human nature. For Chrysippus health, prosperity, a family, things for which a human being normally and properly has a preference, were for the most part correct objects of choice; only in unusual circumstances might his reason tell him that they should be foregone. Epictetus' position was summed up in his slogan *anechou kai apechou*, 'bear and forbear' or 'sustain and abstain'. One must tolerate, as being for the universal good, all those experiences that the world calls misfortunes, and one must not have any emotional attachment to the things that one cannot control. 'Do not admire your wife's beauty and you will not be angry if she is unfaithful'; at life's banquet do not want the dish that is not yet before you and do not try to detain it as it passes away (*Discourses* I. xviii. 11, *Handbook* 15). The orthodox Stoic would not disagree, but constant insistence gives this negative aspect a new emphasis. Not that Epictetus would have admitted his ideal to be a negative one: it was a positive determination to go freely and willingly along with the divine power that ordered all things for the best. This is an aspect not to be forgotten, for if it is overlooked there is a danger of seeing Epictetus as a man who renounces the world, confident in his own self-sufficiency. In fact he completely accepts the world, sure that its goodness is intelligible to its maker. If the individual suffers, his suffering serves a purpose for the universe as a whole, that great city of which he is a member. His reason, being an off-shoot of the universal reason which is God, must approve all that God does. 'What else can I, a lame old man, do but sing a hymn of praise to God? If I were a nightingale, I should do as a nightingale; if I were a swan, I should do as a swan. But now I am a rational being: I must sing the praise of God. This is my work, and I shall not desert this post so long as I am assigned it, and I call on you to join in this same song' (*Discourses* I. 16. 20–1).

Epictetus was able to combine the belief that God is the force shaping all things and constituting all things, including man, with a feeling that he is a person distinct from man. That he found no incompatibility in this combination appears in the following passage:

'Why do you refuse to know whence you have come? When you eat will you not remember who it is that is eating and whom you are feeding? When you go to bed with a woman, who is doing that? When you mix in company, when you take exercise, when you engage in conversation? Don't you know that you are feeding God, exercising God? You carry God around with you, miserable creature, and do not know it. Do you think I mean some god outside you, a god made of silver or gold? No; you carry him within you, and do not perceive that you are defiling him with your unclean thoughts and filthy actions. In the presence of an image of God you would not dare to do any of those things you now do, but in the presence of God himself within you, who watches and hears all, are you not ashamed to entertain these thoughts and do these actions, insensible of your own nature and earning the wrath of God? (*Discourses* II. 8. 11–14).

Whatever the faults of individuals, however widespread was human wickedness, Epictetus insisted that men have a natural capacity for goodness; they are so made that they necessarily acquire a conception of it and must approve what they conceive; if their conception is wrong, they will act wrongly and should be pitied like the lame and the blind; if their conception is put right, they will act rightly and be good men. Secondly, nature has bestowed on them two supporting qualities, *aidôs* and *pistis*. *Aidôs* is the sense of shame that makes a man blush at certain actions and restrains him from wickedness; it is also the feeling of self-respect or respect for the divine element within him. The recognition of *pistis,* the other great human quality, enlarges the horizon; it corrects the emphasis that falls in most of Epictetus' talk on the inner man whom the outer world cannot disturb, for *pistis* is what marks a man's relation to his fellowmen. Epictetus gave the word a new and individual sense, very like that of the Latin *fides,* a virtue central in Roman thought. His Roman hearers will have regarded it as a translation, and for them it will have had an emotive tone. There is no exact English equivalent; it covers reliability, loyalty, and helpfulness; it is the basis on which orderly society is built.

Nature directs all living things to seek what is advantageous to them, but man is unique in that his reason tells him that his advantage lies in acting appropriately towards others. Our first duties are to the family: 'here is your father; it is laid down that you should take care of him, give way to him in everything, put up with his abuse, with his blows. "But he is a bad father!" Did Nature relate you to a good father only? No, simply to a father. "My brother does me wrong!" Then maintain your position with regard to him; do not consider what *he* does, but how *you* must act if your moral purpose is to be what Nature demands.' But duties extend beyond the family, to neighbours, to fellow-citizens, to all mankind. Men are naturally social beings; they love one another and endure one another. To a man who was angered by his slaves' carelessness Epictetus spoke sternly: 'Will you not endure your brother, who has Zeus as his forefather, who is as it were a son born of the same seed as you and begotten like you from above? . . . Do you not remember what you are and to whom you give orders? Your kin, your brothers in nature, the offspring of Zeus. "But I have bought

them, they have not bought me!" You see where you are looking—to the earth, to the pit, to these miserable laws made by
corpses for corpses; you have no eyes for the divine law' (*Discourses* I. 13. 4–5).

To think of all men as one's brothers is a precept that may recall Christianity, of which Epictetus betrays no knowledge. But
love of mankind did not suggest primarily to him the doing of
anything for their physical benefit, and that is only to be expected since he so much depreciated the value of all external
things. His is a love that suffereth all things, but hardly one that
is warm and outgoing, initiating positive aid and support. In
the same way the practical advice that he gives on conduct is
predominantly negative:

> Talk as little as possible; if there is an occasion for talking do
> not talk about sporting events, food and drink, or other
> trivia; above all refrain from blaming, praising, or comparing
> other people; do not laugh much; swear as little as possible;
> avoid dinner-parties; no sex before marriage, but don't boast
> of your chastity or make yourself a nuisance to those who do
> indulge; it is unnecessary to go to the theatre frequently,
> and if you go remain indifferent as to who wins the prize and
> afterwards speak only of the moral profit you have drawn
> from the occasion . . . do not talk at length about your own
> deeds and dangers, for others will be less interested than you;
> avoid raising a laugh, for that diminshes other people's res-
> pect for you. Foul language is dangerous; if it occurs and the
> occasion is suitable, reprove the man who has fallen into it;
> if it is unsuitable, show your displeasure by silence, blushing,
> and frowning. (*Handbook,* c. 33, abbreviated.)

The final sentence here indicates the way in which the Stoic
might best help others, namely by influencing their behaviour
and making them morally better men. This belief, which com-
bines with his depreciation of all those external things that most
men desire or fear, led Epictetus to a sympathy for the Cynics,
or rather for the minority of that numerous body who had
adopted their way of life for the right reasons. There were
many who made the name an excuse for living by begging, with
liberty to abuse the sins of the rich. The true Cynic renounces

169

possessions and children in order to be able to devote himself
without impediment to the work of God, whose messenger he
is. He gives all his energies to the moral education of his fellow
men, without any thought of his own advantage. This is not the
best way of life imaginable, but it is one that is required of those
who are called to it by the wickedness of the world; it is right
for certain individuals here and now, soldiers in the war against
evil (*Discourses* III. 22).

HIEROCLES

A reminder that there were still at this time Stoic philosophers
concerned with theory as well as practice is provided by a papyrus which preserves much of the text of a *Groundwork of Ethics*
by Hierocles, who lived in the early second century AD and is
described by Aulus Gellius as a 'holy and serious man'. He
seems to have worked with inherited material, and is to be
seen as a pillar of orthodoxy. The value of his work lies in showing how Stoic ethics are based on human nature, which is something that develops and changes as the human being grows.

The growth of the embryo, Hierocles begins, is controlled by
the 'nature' within it, a 'breath' which becomes more tenuous
as the time of birth approaches, and so is already on its way
to being converted into *psyche*. The creature that is born is
immediately an *animal,* with sensation and impulse, and it
senses itself. He next digresses by recounting, to establish the
principle that sensation is of self as well as of the outside world,
a large number of stories of animal behaviour. Some seem to
show that the animal is aware of its own strengths and weak-
nesses; others that it is aware of what is dangerous to *it*, e.g.
chickens are not frightened of bulls but of weasels and hawks;
this too implies awareness of self, as does the fact that all other
animals avoid man, perceiving his superiority in reason, i.e. they
compare him with *themselves*. This self-sensation is continuous,
being due to the 'tensional' movement of the *psyche* (cf. p. 77):
the outward movement presses against all parts of the body, the
inward movement towards the controlling centre causes apprehension not only of all parts of the body but also of the apprehending *psyche* itself. (Even in sleep self-sensation is shown by
the way in which we pull the bedclothes over exposed parts and
avoid knocking sore places; a drunkard will clutch his bottle, a

miser his money-bags.) Perception always implies self-awareness; as we perceive something white we also perceive that we are being affected by a white object. All powers that have a controlling function exercise it on themselves; the nature (i.e. breath) that holds a plant together begins by keeping itself together; sensation begins by perceiving itself. The animal, sensing itself, must be pleased, displeased, or indifferent towards the presentation which it has of itself. The two latter alternatives are absurd, as they would lead to its death. Therefore it is pleased; it is made to feel affinity to itself and its constitution (cf. p. 32). Hence animals do all they can to preserve themselves. Infants do not like being shut up in dark silent rooms; the absence of any objects of sensation makes them feel that they are being destroyed. So nurses induce them to shut their eyes, because they are less frightened if they cut off their vision *voluntarily*. (The point is that one's own action is something one feels to belong to one, whereas enforced lack of vision is alien to one's nature. From the time of Antipater at the least Stoics show an interest in child psychology, seeing how the child develops into the man and regarding him as an important agent in that development. The *tendency* of earlier thinkers was to look on him as passive or recalcitrant material for education.) Another sign of the animal's feeling of affinity for itself is the way in which we put up with physical unpleasantness in ourselves that we should find horrid in others.

After this the papyrus becomes very scrappy. The next subject seems to be how with experience the *psyche*'s perception becomes clearer. This may have led on to an argument that as external things are more clearly perceived and at the same time one's own nature is more clearly understood, it is realised that there is an affinity between oneself and some of these external things. Certainly there follows a passage which distinguishes between three kinds of feeling of affinity, that directed towards oneself, that towards one's relatives, and that towards external objects.

An extrapolation of the argument suggests that Hierocles continued by saying that there were further extensions of this feeling of affinity, to include on the one hand all fellow-men and on the other knowledge and all rational, good, and noble conduct. To learn and to be guided by reason are the proper activities of man, whose nature causes him to feel that these things belong to him and are his. Thus morality is to be built on an ever-deepening recognition of what one is, which follows naturally and automatically from widening experience.

MARCUS AURELIUS

Marcus Aurelius, nephew of the emperor Antoninus' wife, was adopted by him when not yet seventeen. He had masters in rhetoric and in philosophy, but at about the age of twenty-five abandoned the former subject. Marked out as he was to be Antoninus' successor, he was much occupied by public duties and had not time for a deep study even of the Stoicism which he embraced. But that philosophy encouraged him in a natural tendency to rule justly and humanely, for it told him that men should help, not harm, one another. At the same time one should not be angry, but bear with transgressors. He was lenient with those guilty of conspiracy against him. In the conduct of trials he was meticulous, even in unimportant cases. Hating bloodshed, he caused gladiators to be given blunted weapons. The local persecutions of Christians during his reign were probably not authorised by him. But although his practical goodness was gratefully recognised by the men of his day, his present reputation rests on the twelve books of *Meditations,* composed probably in the last decade of his life, during which time he was constantly with his armies, fighting off the barbarians along the Danube frontier. Yet they contain almost no reference to these or any other current problems; they are reflections written to support himself in a world that has become dreary and menacing.[1]

The letters that he had written as a young man to Fronto, his

[1] In AD 176, some three years before he died, Marcus made his own son Commodus joint emperor. Previously marked out for the succession, Commodus was then a youth of fifteen. He proved to be a second Nero and his twelve years of rule were disastrous. Did a father's partiality blind the philosopher to his son's defects? Five successive emperors had been chosen, not born to the purple, and all deserved well of the state; why did Marcus not continue this practice? Perhaps he feared that a son, if not chosen to succeed, might be a focus for disaffection; none of his four predecessors had had a son to be considered.

tutor in rhetoric and literature, reveal interest and joy in the world around him; he goes hunting, boasts of climbing a steep hill, visits the antiquities of Anagnia: 'then we worked at gathering the grapes, sweated hard, and were merry . . . then I had a good prattle with my darling mother as she sat on my bed . . . the gong sounded, announcing that my father had gone to the bath-house: so we had dinner after bathing in the oil-press room (I mean dinner after bathing, not bathing in the oil-press room!) and enjoyed listening to the yokels as they ragged one another.' (Fronto, *To Marcus Caesar* 4.4,5,6). Now in the *Meditations* he has become filled with disgust: 'how short-lived and cheap are the objects of our experience, things that can be possessed by a sodomite, a whore, or a brigand. Think next of the characters of those with whom you live; even the best of them can hardly be borne with, not to say that a man can hardly endure himself.' 'What do you see when you take a bath? Oil, sweat, dirt, greasy water, all nauseating. Every part of life is like that.' (V. 10.4, VIII. 24, cf. Seneca *Letter* 107.2.)

Yet he held firm to the belief that everything in the world is the work of a divine Reason, which man must gladly accept and co-operate with; this is the motive for remaining in it: 'why should I live in a world where there are no gods and no Providence?' (II. 11.3.) Yet elsewhere he says that if the world is mere undirected confusion, you should be glad that amidst its breakers you possess within yourself a commanding mind. This independent self cannot be forced to think otherwise than it wishes. 'If you are hurt by anything outside yourself, it is not that which troubles you, but your judgment about it, and that is something you can immediately erase.' The man who concentrates on the goodness of his own commanding element is 'a priest and servant of the gods, using that element seated within him that makes of mere man a being undefiled by pleasures, unwounded by any pain, untouched by any assault, unconscious of any wickedness, a contestant in the greatest of contests, not to be overthrown by any passion, with a deep dye of justice, welcoming with all his heart everything that happens and everything that is assigned to him, and seldom imagining what another man is saying or doing or thinking, and then only if there is some great necessity for so doing to promote the public good.' (III. 4.3.) The element within, which is reason, is a god, as being part of the divine reason that rules the world. We should 'keep the god within us safe from violation or harm, stronger than pleasures and pains, doing nothing without purpose or by mistake or in pretence, having no need that anyone else should do something or not do something, and accepting what happens and what is assigned to us as coming from the same source as that from which it has itself come' (II. 17). This discovery of the god within is common to the Roman Stoics; we have met it in Epictetus (p. 167) and it is to be found in Seneca, who wrote 'God is near you, he is with you, he is within you . . . he treats us as we treat him' (*Letters* 41.3). None of them attempts to meet the obvious psychological difficulty of a self that is one and yet divided. But this is a puzzle presented in many forms; self-knowledge, self-examination and self-love are all familiar; perhaps self-acceptance and self-aversion are experiences of the same kind.

Whereas orthodox Stoicism had regarded the *psyche* as essentially a unity in which the 'command-post' was responsible for all conscious activities except mere sensation, Marcus tends to identify the 'command-post' with reason. Then, instead of dividing man into body and soul, he makes a tripartite division into body, breath, and intelligence, using derogatory diminutives for the first two. This division, whatever its origins may be, is nowhere clearly explained. Breath is the breath of life, which he identifies with the air inhaled and exhaled; but it is also responsible for sensation. Intelligence is contrasted with breath and spoken of with respect, but it would be wrong to suppose that he abandoned the view that reason may be corrupted and turn to error and passion. Yet even corrupted reason can recognise its own corruption, and this may be expressed by saying that there is always a *daimon* within us, a fragment of Zeus, the universal law.

The *Meditations* contain matter of various nature, short extracts from previous authors, summaries of Stoic doctrine, personal reflexions, self-criticism and self-exhortation. Some books have a predominant theme or character, but none is an organised unity except the first, which sets down the moral lessons that Marcus had learned from the teaching or the behaviour of his instructors and his relations, and concludes with thanks to the gods for giving him such teachers, such a family, and the capacity to profit by their lessons. His catalogue of blessings ends as follows:

To have had a frequent clear impression of what life in accord with nature is, with the result that, so far as the gods are concerned and it is a matter of communication, of aid, and of inspiration from heaven, there is no obstacle to my living in accord with nature here and now; that I still fall short of this is due to my own fault and to not observing the reminders, I could almost say the instruction, that comes from the gods. That my body has held out so long in the life I lead. That I did not touch Benedicta or Theodotus [probably slaves], and subsequently again was cured when I fell into the passion of love. That although I was often angry with Rusticus I did nothing that I should have repented. That my mother, who was to die young, spent her last years with me. That whenever I wished to help someone who was in poverty or some other difficulty, I was never told that I had not the money to do it, and that it never happened that I was myself in need of another's help. That my wife is what she is, so obedient, so loving, and so simple.[1] That I had a good supply of suitable persons to bring up my children. That I was granted assistance in dreams, especially against the spitting of blood and dizziness. The answer given me in Caieta: 'what you make of it'. That my love for philosophy did not cause me to fall into the hands of any sophist, or sit down in a corner to analyse syllogisms or become involved in meteorology.

All these things require the help of God and fortune.

Some of Marcus' thoughts might have been expressed by any reflective man, for example:

Do not suppose that because something is hard for yourself to accomplish it is beyond human capacity; but if

[1]Faustina, who bore him thirteen children and died while accompanying him on a journey in the East. Stories of her infidelity and of complicity in the conspiracy of Cassius are probably malicious calumnies.

anything is possible and appropriate for man, think that it is in your reach also. (VI. 19.)

or:

I have often wondered how it is that everyone loves himself more than all other men, but thinks less of his own estimation of himself than he does of that of all others. At any rate, if a god or a wise teacher should stand over a man and tell him to think nothing and contemplate nothing within himself that he will not at the same time speak out to the world, he would not endure that for even a single day. So much do we have more respect for what our neighbours will think of us than for ourselves. (XII. 4.)

Yet more frequently the full meaning can only be grasped if one remembers the Stoic interpretation of the world, and perhaps the majority of the entries are explicitly Stoic in concepts and vocabulary or in their sentiments. A few basic themes recur; Marcus is so convinced of their rightness that they are always fresh and living for him; they are expressed in a hundred different ways. For him the key to life lay in three principles. First, not to admire any of the common objects of ambition, the things which the world thinks valuable. All are as insignificant as man's life, which is but a point in eternity. Second, to accept all that happens, as being part of the divine plan; even the man who repines or resists belongs in fact to that plan. Lastly, to play one's part as a human being in the community: as a Roman and an emperor he had his civic duties to fulfil, as a man he had to love his fellow-men, bear with them, forgive them their faults, teach them, and protect them.

Marcus may not have intended his *Meditations* for any eye but his own. How they were preserved is not known, and the first certain surviving reference to them is in a letter of the learned Arethas written about AD 900. The obscurity which involved them becomes less surprising when one reflects that Marcus was almost the last of the Stoics. A few names are known from the third century, but they are hardly more than names. Even in Marcus' day the shine of half a century's peace and prosperity had departed; plague and barbarian pressure were taking their toll. After him came a century horrid with civil war and barbarian irruption. Stoicism was replaced by philosophies and religions which offered men the consolation of a future life in a better place than this vale of tears.

Among those rivals was Christianity. It had a further advantage as being a religion that offered hope to all, whereas Stoic philosophy was addressed to an *élite*, promising success only to that minority of men who could perfect their reason by their own continued efforts. The Christian was saved by the grace of God and a single act of faith. No sinner was too wicked to repent, no man or woman too simple to believe. Thereafter the Christian might find he must struggle to maintain the standards of conduct expected of him, just as the Stoic struggled to attain the standards he set himself. But the Christian had done what was necessary for salvation and needed only not to throw away his prize of eternal happiness; and he could confidently call for help on a God in whom he had put his trust. The Stoic, relying on himself, could hope neither for complete escape from the pit of wickedness now nor for any reward in a hereafter.

The Christians were well aware of the differences that separated them from the Stoics; above all they criticised the materialism of their psychology and theology and the absence of a transcendent Creator.[1] But when they came to build a philosophy of their own, they had no alternative but to take material where it lay to hand in the thought of the pagans, and they found as much that was suitable among the Stoics as among the Platonists.[2] Often, it must be admitted, they modified the meaning of the vocabulary they took over. Thus for

[1]Generalisations about early Christians must not be understood as being universally true. In a time of active thought not everyone keeps in step. So Tertullian, to take an example, remained a materialist, accepting the Stoic arguments: 'everything that exists is a body of individual quality: only the non-existent is unbodily' (*On the Flesh of Christ* 11).

[2]The Platonists, although never numerous in the period between Marcus Aurelius and Justinian, were tenacious. They had the advantage of a philosophy which found reality outside the material world and which could address itself to intellectual problems, a capacity not evident among the later Stoics.

177

Clement of Alexandria assent is still the first step on the road to knowledge, but it has become an act of will as much as of judgment, and the knowledge to which it can lead depends upon revelation. This is fundamental to his thinking. Philosophy is a preparatory study in which an approach can be made to truth, but in the end truth is only to be had by the direct grasp of what God has revealed.

But much could be assimilated without change. In the first place they accepted the view that the world is the work of God, to be seen as a harmonious unity, determined by his Providence, and designed for the benefit of man. Some of this came also from Jewish sources and from Platonism, but the whole is Stoic, and the arguments for it were drawn mainly from Stoic writing, including those that defended the providential nature of the physical world. Theodicy, or the justification of God, has also to explain the existence of moral evil, and here too the Stoics provided material. Secondly, they concurred in the doctrine that the passions were evil and to be rooted out (but remorse and pity were not to be reckoned among them) and much of the advice on how to overcome them was taken over. Much else in Stoic moralising, of a kind to agree with experience, was welcome, and so the path was easy for converts, like Clement's teacher Pantaenus. Although Stoicism became extinct, the more vital part of its teaching lived on, absorbed and modified in the new religion.

Select Bibliography

I – SOURCES

A. Complete works

The principal works of Cicero (*On the Nature of the Gods, On Divination, On Fate, Academica, Talks at Tusculum, On Duties, De Finibus* or *On Goals in Life*) are satisfactorily translated in the Loeb series, as are those of Seneca and Epictetus. Diogenes Laertius Book 7 and Sextus Empiricus, *Against the Dogmatists* Books 7–11 and *Outlines of Pyrrhonism* Book 3, are less reliably treated. Volume xiii of the Loeb edition of Plutarch's *Moralia*, to contain *On Stoic Self-Contradictions* and *On Common Conceptions* is not yet published.

Among translations of Epictetus those by G. Long (London, Bell, 1877, often reprinted) and P. E. Matheson (Oxford, 1916) can also be recommended. The most reliable translation of Marcus Aurelius is by A. S. L. Farquharson (Oxford, 1944), with commentary.

B. Collections of Fragments

J. ab Arnim (=Hans von Arnim), *Stoicorum Veterum Fragmenta*, 3 vols (Leipzig, Teubner, 1902–5), index volume by M. Adler (ibid., 1925), collects, though not completely, fragments of and references to Stoics down to Antipater, adding many passages to illustrate 'general Stoic doctrine'. The basic collection of texts. A. C. Pearson, *The Fragments of Zeno and Cleanthes* (London, Clay, 1891) has valuable introduction and commentary.

M. van Straaten, *Panétius, sa vie, ses écrits, et sa doctrine avec une édition de ses fragments* (Amsterdam, H. J. Paris, 1946) and *Panaetii Rhodii fragmenta* (Leiden, Brill, 1952; ed. 2, 1962). L. Edelstein and I. G. Kidd, *Posidonius*, vol. i, The Fragments (Cambridge, University Press, 1972) confined to passages which mention Posidonius by name. Vol. ii, a commentary, is in preparation.

THE STOICS

II – Modern works

A. *General*

M. Pohlenz, *Die Stoa,* 2 vols (Göttingen, Vandenhoeck & Ruprecht, 1948), is of outstanding importance. In English there is nothing similar. R. D. Hicks, *Stoic and Epicurean* (London, Longmans Green, 1911), treats some central themes well. E. V. Arnold, *Roman Stoicism* (Cambridge, University Press, 1911, reprinted 1958) is in spite of its title a general history of Stoicism; useful because it quotes texts freely, but unreliable and often misleading. E. Zeller (trans. O. J. Reichel), *The Stoics, Epicureans and Sceptics* (London, Longmans Green, 1892), out of date but still important. E. Bevan, *Stoics and Sceptics* (Oxford, 1913) is brief and stimulating.

A wide range of problems are treated by a number of scholars in A. A. Long, *Problems in Stoicism* (London, Athlone Press, 1971) and by J. M. Rist, *Stoic Philosophy* (Cambridge, University Press, 1969).

B. *Logic*

B. Mates, *Stoic Logic* (Berkeley and Los Angeles, University of California Press, 1953), sets out what is known, emphasises its originality, and translates many texts. W. and M. Kneale, *The Development of Logic* (Oxford, Clarendon Press, 1964) give an appreciative account and try to carry further some of the inquiries begun by the Stoics.

C. *Natural Science*

S. Sambursky, *Physics of the Stoics* (London, Routledge and Kegan Paul, 1959) translates the more important texts; concentrates on what may be seen as anticipations of, or analogues with modern scientific concepts.

D. *Posidonius*

Posidonius has not greatly attracted English scholars, who have welcomed the scepticism of J. F. Dobson, The Posidonius Myth, *Classical Quarterly* 12 (1918) 179 ff. Some aspects are well treated by A. D. Nock, *Journal of Roman Studies* 49 (1959) 1 ff. See also R. M. Jones, *Classical Philology* 21 (1926) 97–113 and 27 (1932) 113–35.

SELECT BIBLIOGRAPHY

E. *Seneca*

The best attempt to give an integrated picture of the man, his life, and his writings is by C. J. Herington, *Arion* 5 (1966), 422–71, reprinted in *Essays on Classical Literature selected from Arion* by N. Rudd (Cambridge, Heffer, and New York, Barnes and Noble, 1972). See also H. MacL. Currie, 'Seneca as Philosopher' in *Neronians and Flavians, Silver Latin I.* ed. D. R. Dudley (London, Routledge and Kegan Paul, 1972) pp. 24–61.

C. W. Mendell, *Our Seneca* (New Haven, Yale University Press, 1941) is an account of Seneca as a dramatist.

F. *Epictetus*

See the excellent book of P. E. More, *Hellenistic Philosophies* (Princeton, 1923) pp. 94–171.

G. *Continuing Influence*

There is much information in R. M. Wenley, *Stoicism and its Influence* (Boston, Marshall Jones, 1924; London, Harrap, 1925) in the series 'Our Debt to Greece and Rome'.

H. *Miscellaneous*

H. C. Baldry, Zeno's Ideal State, *Journal Of Hellenic Studies* 79 (1959) 3–15.

——————, *The Unity of Mankind in Greek Thought* (Cambridge, 1965).

C. O. Brink, Theophrastus and Zeno on Nature and Moral Theory, *Phronesis* i (1955) 123–45.

P. De Lacy, 'The Stoic Categories as Methodological Principles, *Transactions of the American Philological Association* 76 (1945) 246–63.

D. R. Dudley, *A History of Cynicism* (London, Methuen, 1937).

L. Edelstein, *The Meaning of Stoicism* (Cambridge Mass., Harvard University Press, 1966).

J. B. Gould, *The Philosophy of Chrysippus* (Leiden, Brill, 1970).

H. A. K. Hunt, Some Problems in the interpretation of Stoicism, *Journal of the Australasian Universities Language and*

Literature Association 28 (1967) 165–77 (on determinism and free will).

G. B. Kerford, The Search for Personal Identity in Stoic Thought, *Bulletin of the John Rylands Library* 55 (1972) 177–96.

——————, Cicero and Stoic Ethics (in *Cicero and Virgil, Studies in Honour of Harold Hunt*, pp. 60–74).

M. Lapidge, *Phronesis* 18 (1973) 240–78 (on the elements).

A. A. Long, Carneades and the Stoic *Telos*, *Phronesis* 12 (1967) 59–90.

——————, *Hellenistic Philosophy* (London, Duckworth, 1974), supplies an up-to-date and scholarly account.

——————, The Stoic Concept of Evil, *Philosophical Quarterly* 18 (1968) 329–43.

——————, Aristotle's Legacy to Stoic Ethics, *Bulletin of the Institute of Classical Studies*, 15 (1968) 72–85.

C. E. Manning, Seneca and the Stoics on the Equality of the Sexes, *Mnemosyne* 26 (series iv) (1973) 170–7.

G. Murray, The Stoic Philosophy, in *Essays and Addresses* (London, Allen and Unwin, 1921).

M. E. Reesor, The Stoic Concept of Quality, *American Journal of Philology* 75 (1954) 40–58.

——————, The Stoic Categories, ibid. 78 (1957) 63–82.

——————, Fate and Possibility in Early Stoic Philosophy, *Phoenix* 19 (1965) 285–97.

F. Solmsen, *Cleanthes or Posidonius? The Basis of Stoic Physics* (Amsterdam, 1961).

G. R. Stanton, The cosmopolitan Ideas of Epictetus and Marcus Aurelius, *Phronesis* 13 (1968) 183–95.

R. B. Todd, The Stoic Common Notions, *Symbolae Osloenses* 48 (1973) 47–75.

J. M. C. Toynbee, Dictators and Philosophers in the First Century AD, *Greece and Rome* 13 (1944) 43–58.

G. Watson, *The Stoic Theory of knowledge* (Belfast 1966).

C. Wirszubski, *Libertas as a Political Ideal at Rome during the late Republic and Early Principate*, pp. 138–53 (Cambridge, 1950).

Glossary

For the benefit of readers who may refer to Greek or Latin texts there are here set out a number of technical terms or words used by Stoics in a peculiar restricted sense together with the equivalents adopted by authors who wrote in Latin.

arete	honestas, uirtus	virtue
agathon, spoudaion	bonum	good
kalon	honestum	beautiful, fine
haireton	expetendum	to be sought for
chrêsimon, ôphelimon, sympheron	utile	useful, beneficial
kakon, phaulon	malum	bad
aischron	turpe	ugly, shameful
pheukton	fugiendum	to be shunned
blaberon	nocens	harmful
kakiâ	uitium	badness, vice
adiaphora	indifferentia	indifferent a. morally b. absolutely
proêgmenon	productum, promotum, praepositum	having precedence
lêpton, lekton	sumendum, eligendum	to be chosen, preferable
euchrêston	commodum	serviceable
apoproêgmenon	reiectum, remotum	relegated
alêpton	reiciendum	not to be chosen
dyschrêston	incommodum	unserviceable
axiân echon	aestimabile	having worth or value
apaxiân echon	inaestimabile	having unworth
kathêkon	officium	appropriate action
katorthôma	recte factum	correct action
hamartêma	praue factum	incorrect action

Index

In transliterated words a final letter *e* is always to be pronounced as a long vowel. Thus *arete* is a word of three syllables, *psyche* one of two. Other instances of long *e* have been marked with a circumflex, as have those of long *a* and long *o*.

INDEX

INDEX